Additional Praise for Moral Formation and the Virtuous Life

"This book wonderfully captures the theological, historical, and communal contours of moral formation in early Christian thought. The introduction to each section is nuanced but accessible, aptly identifying and spelling out the crucial issues and thinkers. The range of coverage is diverse, exemplary, and fitting. The tone of the book is refreshingly astute in its selection of texts and its constructive promise."
—Fred Aquino, Abilene Christian University

"What it means to live a good life is today perhaps more contested than ever before. The early church had a clear and distinctive teaching on this subject. Despite the passage of two millennia, it is still capable of speaking to us today. This collection of texts makes the early Christian heritage of moral and spiritual wisdom accessible to all."
—David Bradshaw, University of Kentucky

Moral Formation and the Virtuous Life

Moral Formation and the Virtuous Life

PAUL M. BLOWERS, VOLUME EDITOR

FORTRESS PRESS
MINNEAPOLIS

MORAL FORMATION AND THE VIRTUOUS LIFE

Copyright © 2019 Fortress Press. All rights reserved. Except for brief quotations in critical articles or reviews, no part of this book may be reproduced in any manner without prior written permission from the publisher. Email copyright@fortresspress.com or write to Permissions, Fortress Press, PO Box 1209, Minneapolis, MN 55440-1209.

Cover image: IStock Blessing Christ in the Apse, St Paul Basilica, Rome, by faulk74
Cover design: Alisha Lofgren

Print ISBN: 978-1-4514-9634-5
eBook ISBN: 978-1-5064-5737-6

Contents

	Series Foreword	xi
	Introduction	1
1.	The Anatomy and Scope of Repentance	13
2.	Resisting Worldly Powers and Renouncing Worldly Evils	35
3.	Christianity as a Rule of Life	49
4.	Divine Paideia and the Quest for Moral Wisdom	69
5.	Biblical Narrative, Hagiography, and Moral Mimesis	99
6.	Sacraments, Liturgy, and Moral Formation	119
7.	Habituating Virtues and Eradicating Vices	137
8.	Love: Beginning and End of the Christian Virtues	155
	Supplemental Bibliography	183
	Index of Subjects and Names	191
	Index of Scriptural References	199

Series Foreword

In his book *The Spirit of Early Christian Thought*, Robert Louis Wilken reminds us that "Christianity is more than a set of devotional practices and a moral code: it is also a way of thinking about God, about human beings, about the world and history."[1] From its earliest times, Wilken notes, Christianity has been inescapably ritualistic, uncompromisingly moral, and unapologetically intellectual.

Christianity is deeply rooted in history and continues to be nourished by the past. The ground of its being and the basis of its existence is the life of a historic person, Jesus of Nazareth, whom Christians identify as God's unique, historical act of self-communication. Jesus presented himself within the context of the history of the people of Israel, and the earliest disciples understood him to be the culmination of that history, ushering in a new chapter in God's ongoing engagement with the world.

The crucial period of the first few centuries of Christianity is known as the patristic era or the time of the church fathers. Beginning after the books of the New Testament were written and continuing until the dawn of the Middle Ages (ca. 100–700 CE), this period encompasses a large and diverse company of thinkers and personalities. Some came from Greece and Asia Minor, others from Palestine and Egypt, and still others from Spain, Italy, North Africa, Syria, and present-day Iraq. Some

---

1. Robert Louis Wilken, *The Spirit of Early Christian Thought: Seeking the Face of God* (New Haven: Yale University Press, 2003), xiii.

wrote in Greek, others in Latin, and others in Syriac, Coptic, Armenian, and other languages.

This is the period during which options of belief and practice were accepted or rejected. Christian teachers and thinkers forged the language to express Christian belief clearly and precisely; they oversaw the life of the Christian people in worship and communal structure; and they clarified and applied the worshiping community's moral norms.

Every generation of Christians that has reconsidered the adequacy of its practice and witness and has reflected seriously on what Christians confess and teach has come to recognize the church fathers as a precious inheritance and source for instruction and illumination. After the New Testament, no body of Christian literature has laid greater claim on Christians as a whole.

The purpose of this series is to invite readers "to return to the sources," to discover firsthand the riches of the common Christian tradition and to gain a deeper understanding of the faith and practices of early Christianity. When we recognize how Christian faith and practices developed through time, we also appreciate how Christianity still reflects the events, thoughts, and social conditions of this earlier history.

Ad Fontes: Sources of Early Christian Thought makes foundational texts accessible through modern, readable English translations and brief introductions that lay out the context of these documents. Each volume brings together the best recent scholarship on the topic and gives voice to varying points of view to illustrate the diversity of early Christian thought. Entire writings or sections of writings are provided to allow the reader to see the context and flow of the argument.

Together, these texts not only chronicle how Christian faith and practice came to adopt its basic shape but also summon contemporary readers to consider how the events, insights, and social conditions of the early church continue to inform Christianity in the twenty-first century.

George Kalantzis
Series Editor

Introduction

One of the monumental legacies of the early church in its witness to later centuries of Christians is the conviction that a Christian is formed over time through multiple means and disciplines, and not simply validated in a single, momentary act of obedience or intellectual assent. This is not to suggest that specific acts of obedience to divine commandments or mindful adherence to the church's doctrinal claims played no role in confirming one as a Christian; rather, it means that Christian identity was bound up with the dynamics of ongoing growth in discipleship at the different levels—emotional, intellectual, intuitive or aesthetic, behavioral, and so on—at which a believer was called to maturity, "to the measure of the stature of the fullness of Christ" (Eph 4:13).

Already the book of Acts evidences the incipient temptation among some Jewish Christian authorities in the primitive Jerusalem church to ground Christian identity "nomically" in particular laws or commandments (Acts 15:1); and later we see, among gentile congregations, the lure of anchoring that identity in a particular hero cult (1 Cor 1:11–13) or in an exclusive and allegedly superior "knowledge" (*gnōsis*, 1 Tim 6:20). In principle, however, nothing was to usurp the authority of "Christ crucified" in delineating the terms of Christian identity—an authority that, given Christ's material absence, could only find expression through a strong consensus among the churches on their canon of Scripture, their doctrinal rule of faith, and their identity-defining practices.

Meanwhile the expansion of Christianity in the Roman world in the pre-Constantinian age, marked by the multiple social and cultural battles that the new faith confronted as an alleged *superstitio* and officially illegal religion (*religio illicita*),[1] precipitated internal and external crises that greatly heightened the stakes of Christian self-definition. These struggles also tested the solidarity and viability of whole communities and not just the religious identity or fidelity of their individual members. In his study *The Rise of Normative Christianity*, Arland Hultgren has cogently proposed that the crucial factor enabling early Christian communities to survive, thrive, and network with each other in the direction of a shared, normative identity was their respective capacities to achieve congruence between their theological worldview and their moral ethos. In a word, their practices had to be consistently informed by, and concretely embody, their core convictions regarding God, Jesus Christ, creation, humanity, sin, and the destiny of the world.[2] Vital to this process was a Christian community's rehearsal of the larger sacred narrative into which it believed itself to have been engrafted, and which it determined to play out in its own time and context.[3] Thus a significant task of Christian protagonists and apologists in the first three centuries was to instill in the faithful the consciousness of a shared past, such as could be recounted and in some sense relived through engagement with Scripture and through the sacred remembrance and reinforcement operative in sacramental and liturgical rituals. This meant nurturing a collective moral memory—and conscience—that provided the bearings and rationale for Christians' common practices and ethical commitments. Immanuel Kant's influential modern profile of the human being

---

1. On these struggles, see especially Robert Wilken, *The Christians as the Romans Saw Them*, 2nd ed. (New Haven: Yale University Press, 2003); and Stephen Benko, *Pagan Rome and the Early Christians* (Bloomington: Indiana University Press, 1984).

2. *The Rise of Normative Christianity* (Minneapolis: Fortress Press, 1994), 20–80; cf. also Wayne Meeks, *The First Urban Christians: The Social World of the Apostle Paul* (New Haven: Yale University Press, 1983), 164–92; *The Moral World of the First Christians*, Library of Early Christianity 6 (Philadelphia: Westminster, 1986), 97–160; J. Ian McDonald, *The Crucible of Christian Morality* (London: Routledge, 1998), 85–122.

3. On this commanding "moral story," see Wayne Meeks, *The Origins of Christian Morality* (New Haven: Yale University Press, 1993), 189–210.

as an autonomous subject, fully owning and commanding her or his will and exercising moral reason in reference to an objective categorical imperative, stands in rather sharp contrast with ancient Christian thinking on morality and ethics, where the emphasis was less on an individual's moral decision-making or "situational" ethics and more on communal moral vision shaping each believer's moral conscience and ethical horizon.[4]

In the texts presented in this book, the reader will hopefully gain a better sense of exactly what this communal shaping process entailed. Experientially and practically, it was a matter of sustained pastoral instruction and admonition; sacramental initiation (baptism) and reincorporation (Eucharist); liturgical "replay" of Christianity's sacred history; and learned ethical behaviors in a communal context where Christians faced many shared moral challenges. These challenges included not just qualms of private personal conscience but open controversy over many issues (e.g., sexual ethics, marriage and celibacy, wealth and poverty); ethnic conflict; the attraction and utility of pagan learning; the lures of pagan entertainment; participation in the military or in civil service roles in Roman government; and much more. These issues demand volumes and primary readings of their own. The readings in later chapters will focus rather on moral formation itself, the disciplines indispensable to preparing the Christian to face these ethical challenges and even thrive in their midst. Needless to say, *moral* development was hardly segregated from the overall religious formation of the Christian. Numerous early Christian authors conceded that their pagan neighbors were already quite capable of being morally astute—indeed, these authors borrowed abundantly from revered traditions of Greco-Roman moral philosophy—but Christians were to be a people set apart, distinguished by redeemed life "in Christ" (cf. Rom 3:24; 6:11, 23; 8:1–2, 39; 12:5; 16:3, 7; 1 Cor 1:30; 4:10, 15, 17) and by their continuing embodiment of Christ himself in the world.[5]

Other than rare autobiographical compositions like Augus-

---

4. On communal "moral vision" in its various incipient forms in the apostolic period, see Richard Hays, *The Moral Vision of the New Testament: Community, Cross, New Creation* (San Francisco: HarperCollins, 1996).
5. On some of these, see Meeks, *Moral World of the First Christians*, 40–64.

tine's *Confessions* or much of the poetry of the Cappadocian bishop Gregory of Nazianzus, fairly few early Christian texts provide us with personal, intimate portraits of a believer's moral or spiritual formation. We must therefore extrapolate aspects of this process from a broad variety of texts that were part of the grand literary and discursive transformation that accompanied the growth of Christianity before and especially after Constantine.[6] The texts that I am excerpting in this anthology come from an amazing array of literary genres: letters, sermons, biblical commentaries and homilies, didactic and disciplinary writings, apologies, hagiography, orations of various kinds (protreptic, encomiastic, etc.), theological treatises, and monastic sapiential works. I have nevertheless organized the textual specimens not by literary or rhetorical genre but according to themes that highlight some of the most important dimensions and modes of Christian moral formation. At the beginning of each chapter, I will expand briefly on its proper theme and introduce the representative texts that I have selected, realizing all the while that for each individual text, there were often many others that merited inclusion. My goal has been to choose writers and works that bring unique insight from within their own times and peculiar contexts, though frequently they will reveal overlapping perspectives.

Let me say a word, then, about unity amid the diversity of these texts. Much ground is covered in them, but I would alert the reader to certain integrating themes that run across the chapters and that we can consider properly basic to early Christian moral instruction.

MIMESIS AND EXEMPLA

For the early churches, Christian morality was neither merely dictated by experts nor reduced to an exclusive, exhaustive list of behavioral axioms. Rather, it was inculcated over the course of time as believers were admonished to imitate paragons of moral excellence. Even today, educational psychologists insist that we

---

6. See the analysis of this transformation in Averil Cameron, *Christianity and the Rhetoric of Empire* (Berkeley: University of California Press, 1991).

learn by imitation; it is a fact of human development beginning in infancy. But the ancients were already well aware of this. As Robert Wilken observes, the dispensing of moral wisdom early on did indeed include commandments or precepts for Christian performance, of which we find many in the New Testament itself; but often they were couched in the examples of antecedent heroic figures who obeyed those precepts in specific circumstances.[7] When Paul says, "Be imitators of me, as I am of Christ" (1 Cor 11:1 RSV), he knows full well that his directive carries little force apart from the example of his life over the long haul, his sufferings for Christ, and his faithfulness annealed in the refiner's fire of experience and hard testing (cf. 2 Cor 4:1–5:21; 11:16–33). Prescriptivism, or bare obedience to Christ, was not, then, the final goal of Christian moral formation so much as the internalizing of sustained, virtuous habits of thinking and acting. Reliance on vivid examples of Christian virtue (and negative examples of vice) will show up in many of the selected texts in later chapters.

But as Wilken further notes, biblical exempla were often appropriated merely as moral "types" in early Christianity (e.g., the faithful or "prudent" Abraham, the "patient" Job, etc.). Only later, with the emergent literature of martyrs—*Acts* and *Lives* of saints—especially from the fourth and fifth centuries on, do we find extensive hagiographies that celebrated significant Christian figures who were themselves imitators of the biblical saints. The growing liturgical cult of the saints promoted popular devotion to these figures and served to sustain vivid profiles of their virtue and fidelity in the church's collective memory. These figures, though eulogized in the literature, were less "sanitized by tradition" and more approachable in their humanity, and they revealed the complexion of Christian character, not just individual virtues.[8]

---

7. Robert Louis Wilken, "The Lives of the Saints and the Pursuit of Virtue," in *Remembering the Christian Past* (Grand Rapids: Eerdmans, 1995), 125–26.
8. See Wilken's discussion in "The Lives of the Saints and the Pursuit of Virtue," 126–44.

CHRISTIAN *PHILOSOPHIA*: CONTEMPLATION AND PRACTICE

Early Christian appropriation of conventions and terminology from classical and Hellenistic-Roman moral philosophy is extensive and well-documented, but among the more pervasive and enduring carryovers in patristic moral thought is the pairing of the disciplines of "contemplation" (Greek *theōria*; Latin *contemplatio*) and "practice" (Greek *praxis*; Latin *actus*, later *praxis*). "Theory and practice" is, of course, a commonplace today in many arts and sciences, but the tandem has a much more precise meaning in antiquity, where philosophical schools debated whether the elevated pursuit of divine realities through contemplation or the active disciplines of moral practice should carry the day.[9] Inevitably the two could not live without each other, especially in the Christian tradition, as erudite writers like Clement of Alexandria and Origen inseminated this tandem in Christian usage. It took on a whole life of its own in monastic circles, with sages such as Evagrius of Pontus and John Cassian laboring to integrate the contemplative and practical dimensions of the monk's regimen.

"Contemplation" as such retained the sense of striving after spiritual truth, and the term *theōria* even became a byword for interpreting the heights and depths of Scripture. But it could also simply convey moral "vision" in the broad sense, the need for Christians to consistently "see" the larger framework of their moral and spiritual vocation in the light of God's salvific economy and judgment as centered in Jesus Christ. At the level of moral practice, then, it meant the capacity to reflect on one's dispositions and actions, for which reason contemplative virtues like prudence (one of the four "cardinal" virtues in antiquity) were regularly paired with more pragmatic or ascetic virtues like self-control and almsgiving. Patristic and monastic writers, especially from the fourth century on, also regularly referred to the

---

9. See Thomas Bénatouïl and Mauro Bonazzi, "θεωρία and βίος θεωρητικός from the Presocratics to the End of Late Antiquity: An Overview," in Theoria, Praxis and the Contemplative Life after Plato and Aristotle, ed. Thomas Bénatouïl and Mauro Bonazzi (Leiden: Brill, 2012), 1–14.

overarching ideal of Christian *philosophia* in the same manner that the philosophical schools sought to inculcate their principles in particular ways of life. *Philosophia* came to mean an ever-maturing discipleship and a moral wisdom-in-action suited to monastics and non-monastics alike. The historical fact of the matter, however, is that monastic theologians (e.g., Evagrius of Pontus, John Cassian, Benedict, Maximus), some of whom became bishops (e.g., John Chrysostom, Gregory the Great), increasingly played the most prolific role in articulating the language of moral discipline and progress in the early church. Even influential bishops like the Cappadocian Fathers (Basil of Caesarea, Gregory of Nazianzus, and Gregory of Nyssa) and Augustine were ascetics who thoroughly promoted this vision of Christian life as christocentric *philosophia*.

VIRTUES AND VICES

Patristic moralists, broadly speaking, found significant inspiration in the "virtue ethics" that descended especially from Aristotle and that found traction in the philosophical schools and in Hellenistic Jewish moral traditions as well as in the New Testament and sub-apostolic sources.[10] Its place in the New Testament is enshrined, for example, in Paul's statement in Philippians 4:8: "At last, brothers and sisters, whatever is true, whatever honorable, whatever just, whatever pure, whatever pleasing, whatever kindly-disposed, whatever auspicious, if there is any virtue [*aretē*] and anything worthy of praise—focus your thinking on these things."

Virtue was about moral virtuosity and excellence, and the formation of the Christian in virtue depended not just on conditioned behavior but more basically on healthy, engrained dispositions and habits of mind and soul. Indeed, instilling virtues was about orienting one's entire moral self to salutary ends as determined by the gospel and the church's teaching. Already with

10. For background, see McDonald, *Crucible of Christian Morality*, 180–206. On the legacy of Aristotelian virtue ethics, see esp. Alasdair MacIntyre, *After Virtue: A Study in Moral Theory*, 3rd ed. (Notre Dame, IN: University of Notre Dame Press, 2007).

Aristotle, as Rosiland Hursthouse remarks, "The virtues (and vices) are all dispositions not only to act, but to feel emotions, as reactions as well as impulses to action.... In the person with the virtues, these emotions will be felt on the *right* occasion, toward the *right* people or objects, for the *right* reasons."[11] This observation is especially apropos of early Christian moral teaching, since many of what became Christian "virtues" appear to us as principled emotions (e.g., mercy, patience, humility, etc.), just as what became "vices" appear as destructive emotions or "passions" (e.g., envy, pride, wrath, etc.). Christianity readjusted the goal of virtue away from a *happiness* (*eudaimonia*) defined on purely Aristotelian terms and from the public *honor* cherished in Greek and Roman society, as its focus had to be christomorphic and self-sacrificial in response to divine (incarnational) grace; but its apparatus stayed much the same: the cultivation of *character* in terms both of virtues of mind and properly ethical virtues.

Conversely, a Christian's growth in the virtues necessarily entailed diligent uprooting of the vices. Generally speaking, the early church had little use for considering sin in purely abstract terms. Even Augustine's classic doctrine of "original" sin, which has had such an influential afterlife in Western Christianity, was not intended to drift into abstraction, since that hereditary sin still manifested itself in specific vices, especially lust (*concupiscentia*), in Augustine's view. Sin was *concrete* disobedience of God's will, an offense to his mercy and goodness, for which reason, from very early on, patristic and monastic theologians speculated on the original *vice* in Eden (pride? envy? self-love?) that precipitated the fall of humanity. Meanwhile the quest to inculcate the Christian virtues was *ipso facto* a moral and spiritual battle against the deadly allure of the vices, and indeed, identifying the most detrimental vices was half of that battle. Here too it was monastic authors, some of whom juxtaposed the most damaging vices with the most edifying virtues, who proved remarkably insightful in portraying Christians' moral formation.

---

11. Rosiland Hursthouse, *On Virtue Ethics* (Oxford: Oxford University Press, 1999), 108.

THEOLOGICAL ANTHROPOLOGY AND MORAL PSYCHOLOGY

In approaching the texts selected for this anthology, I advise the reader to keep in mind that virtually all of them carry implicit and explicit assumptions about human nature and human moral agency. "Moral theology" and "theological ethics" are relatively recent terms, but they work well in describing the intention of many early Christian moralists who, like their modern counterparts, hoped to frame the Christian life as an embodiment of particular doctrinal commitments, including commitments of theological anthropology. For example, a strong assumption for these authors is that a human being is uniquely created in the image of God (Gen 1:26–27) and thus endowed, ontologically, with a likeness to God needing to be nurtured and perfected. Some patristic interpreters, beginning with Irenaeus of Lyons, Clement of Alexandria, and Origen, even proposed to distinguish between the "image" (*eikōn*; *imago*) of God, as a natural gift to the human creature, and "likeness" (*homoiōsis*; *similitudo*) as the product of a lifelong process of assimilation to God's own virtues and perfection. The latter was taken up into developing notions of human deification, whereby salvation itself was a progress in imaging God, or imaging Christ, the true Image, "from one degree of glory to another" (2 Cor 3:6).

In addition, as Christian thinkers increasingly reflected on the capacity of human beings for moral growth and their potential for perfection, they also developed a "moral psychology," a theory of how the mind and soul are uniquely outfitted, as it were, for projecting salutary moral ends, cultivating virtues, and putting those virtues into practice. Many Christian writers, especially in the monastic tradition, adopted a basically Platonic understanding of the tripartite soul—famous from Plato's allegory of reason as the "charioteer" reining in two "race horses," the lower drives of desire (*epithymia*) and "temper" (*thymos*)—which must not merely be tamed or controlled but also recruited to sound purposes.[12] Other writers were drawn to the Stoic psychology wherein the mind was a "ruling principle"

---

12. See *Phaedrus* 246A–254E.

(*hēgemonikon*) directing the soul's subordinate faculties, exercising them in morally healthy ways. Some Christian writers found ways to combine these and other philosophical ideas while adding their own accents and insights and drawing on biblical perspectives (e.g., Paul's definition of the human being as a trinity of mind [spirit], soul, and body; or the deeply rooted notion of "the heart" as the seat of one's morality and piety).

Interestingly, the concept of "the will" as a unique faculty of moral agency appears to have been a Christian invention. What we would call "willing" was understood by many Greco-Roman philosophers principally as a function of intellect—especially Aristotle, with his idea of "rational desire," the combination of intellect and appetite that is necessary for motivating action, moral and otherwise. In the Western Christian tradition, Augustine is credited with isolating the will (*voluntas*) as a faculty of its own, the instrument par excellence of a sinner's response to the saving God—even though sin, in his view, had rendered the will disabled and in need of liberation by grace.[13] In the East, Maximus the Confessor looked to fortify and stabilize the principle of an individual's moral deliberation (*gnōmē*) by fusing it to what he called "natural will": the human will (*thelēma*) in its inherent predisposition toward its Creator and as perfectly instantiated in Jesus Christ.[14] While differences certainly appeared among Christian authors West and East over what constituted "free will," there was ultimate consensus that the human will is only truly free to the extent that it virtuously conforms to the will of God.

Going forward, there are certainly other important themes and emphases that flow through the diverse texts that fill up the chapters of this book. Some of these will be addressed in the

13. For analysis of Augustine's invention of the will, see Albrecht Dihle, *The Theory of Will in Classical Antiquity* (Berkeley: University of California Press, 1982), 123–44.

14. For background on Maximus's views of human will, see Paul Blowers, *Maximus the Confessor: Jesus Christ and the Transfiguration of the World* (Oxford: Oxford University Press, 2016), 121, 123–24, 159–65, 213, 217; also Richard Sorabji, *Emotion and Peace of Mind: From Stoic Agitation to Christian Temptation* (Oxford: Oxford University Press, 2000), 337–40; "The Concept of the Will from Plato to Maximus the Confessor," in *The Will and Human Action: From Antiquity to the Present Day*, ed. Thomas Pink and M. W. F. Stone (London: Routledge, 2004), 20–22.

chapter introductions. The texts on their own, however, will doubtless invite discussion of the frameworks, principles, constitutive disciplines, and ultimate objectives of moral formation and the virtuous life in early Christianity.

A NOTE ON THE TRANSLATIONS

The translations in the chapters are of three kinds. Several are my own, based on the best available critical editions of the Greek or Latin texts; thus where another translator is not named, the translation is mine. In some cases I have used dated translations, such as those in the Ante-Nicene Fathers and the Nicene and Post-Nicene Fathers series (nineteenth century), excerpts from which I have revised and updated. In other cases, I have reproduced preexisting recent translations of excellent quality, permissions for which will be duly noted. On some occasions I have taken the liberty to modify preexisting translations for the sake of more gender-inclusive language, unless it does not fit the context or becomes grammatically awkward.

1.

The Anatomy and Scope of Repentance

INTRODUCTION

Repentance was, and is, both the threshold and the fulcrum of a Christian's moral and spiritual formation. What the New Testament calls a *metanoia* is a watershed change of mind, heart, perspective, and life. As Wayne Meeks emphasizes, "Early Christianity was a movement of converts. That is, the Christians thought of themselves as people who had turned their lives around, from one state to another profoundly better."[1] Such was not momentary, however, but a whole process that entailed agonizing reappraisal of one's past sins, a contrition that did not abruptly end at the river or font where one was baptized for the remission of those sins (Acts 2:38).

An early crisis for the churches of the second and third centuries therefore centered on determining whether the repentance connected with baptism was sufficient in itself or, because believers continued to sin (sometimes gravely) after baptism, further repentance was prospectively warranted to ensure the grace of forgiveness. The *Shepherd of Hermas* [1.1.1], an anonymous Jewish Christian apocalyptic and homiletic text of the second century, not only indicates the abiding importance of straightforward commandments or "mandates" in the grammar

---

1. Meeks, *Origins of Christian Morality*, 18.

of Christian moral instruction but also witnesses to the fairly prevalent view that after baptism, a Christian only had the possibility of one last, or "second," repentance. This ostensible rigorism makes sense in a context where the churches were acutely aware of the damaging effect of grievous sin or apostasy after baptism on the integrity, solidarity, and public face of Christian communities. The Carthaginian Christian lawyer Tertullian (ca. 155–ca. 240) confirms that the "second repentance" was assumed doctrine in the North African churches but adds that it was to be followed up with a public confession (*exomologēsis*) of the postbaptismal sin, which would provide the appropriate cleansing of the offender's conscience and stand that person on new moral ground [1.1.2]. Here was an initial signal of the sacramentalization of penance in early and medieval Christianity. But the difficulties of upholding such rigor were obvious. Was a "last chance" repentance consistent with apostolic teaching? Was it pastorally sound? Lactantius (ca. 250–ca. 325), a Christian apologist and the tutor of Constantine's eldest son, indicates a more realistic and mitigating position, calling repentance a continuing "medicine" ever effective for restoring the Christian to her or his moral senses [1.1.3].

Other early Christian authorities routinely prescribed repentance as a lifelong discipline, a perennial follow-up to conversion. The prolific episcopal preacher and moralist John Chrysostom (ca. 347–407), in Antioch and then in Constantinople, regularly upheld repentance as a mainstay of Christian piety [1.2.1]. Monastics sages did the same, like the east-Syrian monk Pseudo-Macarius (fourth century) and his later devotee Mark the Monk (fifth century), who battled against certain ascetic idealists convinced that baptismal grace was ineffectual to cancel sin but that a monk, through rigorous asceticism, could arrive at a state of spiritual perfection whereupon repentance was irrelevant. For Pseudo-Macarius, repentance was a mark of continuing cooperation with God's saving grace, allowing no room for complacence [1.2.2], while Mark insisted that baptismal grace was definitive but also had continuing efficacy in the life of the Christian who progressed in repentance [1.2.3]. The message was the same: no one, even the allegedly perfect, outgrows repentance. In the West, Augustine (354–430) too redefined the "second" repentance as "perpetual supplication throughout the whole of this life," a sign of the sinner's constant need for grace [1.2.4].

Monastic sages, in particular, contributed to understanding Christian repentance as having a strong component of compunction and godly tears, the deep sorrow over one's sin that was key to cleansing the moral conscience and recommitting oneself to new life in Christ. When veteran elder monks of the Egyptian desert [1.3.1] in the fourth and fifth centuries, and seasoned monastic theologians like Evagrius of Pontus (345–399) and John Cassian (ca. 365–ca. 433), spoke of repentance as compunction [1.3.2; 1.3.3], they were not describing a momentary sadness or temporary pang of guilt; rather, they were recommending a more primal contrition, the shedding again and again of Adam's own tears, as it were, in the recognition that the whole human race was caught up in the tragedy of sin and that radical repentance was the only way forward toward transformation. The Syrian bishop and accomplished preacher Jacob of Sarug (ca. 451–521) found exactly the model he wanted of such compunction in the "sinful woman," who magnificently combined oil and tears in washing Jesus's feet [1.3.4].

As the post-Constantinian church entered awkwardly into a new era of political amnesty and increasing imperial patronage, with the threat of superficial allegiance to Christianity an inevitable concern, episcopal preachers responded not only by invoking the Christian public to more intensive moral self-awareness and discipline (a hallmark of John Chrysostom's preaching) but also pressing to assure that the churches would host and nurture public and private penitence. A full-fledged sacrament of penance was now in the making. Ambrose of Milan (339–397) and the later Gallican bishop Caesarius of Arles (ca. 470–542) strongly encouraged public repentance as vital to the Church's ministry of reconciliation. "Let the Church, our Mother, weep for you," writes Ambrose, "and wash away your guilt with her tears" [1.4.1]. Caesarius intends for the humiliation of public penitence to be matched by the onlooking congregants' show of mercy and solidarity with those who, like them, have fallen from grace and need cleansing and restoration

[1.4.2]. The ideal was for the whole congregation to enfold penitents in its bosom and to build them up again in the body of Christ.

THE TEXTS

1.1 The "Second Repentance"

1.1.1 *Shepherd of Hermas*, Commandment 4[2]

3. And I said to him, "I should like to continue my questions." "Speak on," he said. And I said, "I heard, sir, some teachers maintain that there is no other repentance than that which takes place when we descended into the water [in baptism] and received remission of our former sins" (cf. Acts 2:38). He said to me, "That was sound doctrine which you heard; for that is really the case. For whoever has received remission of sins ought not to sin anymore, but to live in purity. Since, however, you inquire diligently into all things, I will point this also out to you, not as giving occasion for error to those who are to believe, or have lately believed, in the Lord. For those who have now believed, and those who are to believe, have not repentance for their sins; but they have remission of their previous sins. For to those who have been called before these days, the Lord has set repentance. For the Lord, knowing the heart, and foreknowing all things, knew the weakness of human being and the manifold wiles of the Devil, that he would inflict some evil on the servants of God, and would act wickedly towards them. The Lord, therefore, being merciful, has had mercy on the work of his hand, and has set repentance for them; and he has entrusted to me power over this repentance. And therefore I say to you, that if any one is tempted by the Devil, and sins after that great and holy calling in which the Lord has called his people to everlasting life, that person has opportunity to repent only once. But if he or she should sin frequently after this, and then repent, for such a per-

---

2. Translated by F. Crombie, *Fathers of the Second Century*, Ante-Nicene Fathers, vol. 2 (Edinburgh: T&T Clark, 1885), 22. Revised and updated.

son repentance will be of no avail; for with difficulty will he or she live." And I said, "Sir, I feel that life has come back to me in listening attentively to these commandments; for I know that I shall be saved, if in future I sin no more." And he said, "You will be saved, you and all who keep these commandments."

4. And again I asked him, saying, "Sir, since you have been so patient in listening to me, will you show me this also?" "Speak," said he. And I said, "If a wife or husband die, and the widower or widow marry, does he or she commit sin?" "There is no sin in marrying again," said he; "but if they remain unmarried, they gain greater honor and glory with the Lord (cf. 1 Cor 7:8); but if they marry, they do not sin. Guard, therefore, your chastity and purity, and you will live to God. What commandments I now give you, and what I am to give, keep from henceforth, yea, from the very day when you were entrusted to me, and I will dwell in your house. And your former sins will be forgiven, if you keep my commandments. And all shall be forgiven those who keep these my commandments, and walk in this chastity."

1.1.2 Tertullian, *On Repentance*[3]

9. Since, then, this second and one last repentance is so strict a matter, the proving of it must be proportionately rigorous, such that it is not merely manifested in the conscience but also in some external act. This act is better expressed in its common Greek usage as the *exomologēsis*, wherewith we confess our wrongdoing to the Lord, not as if he did not already know it, but insofar as the satisfaction [for the sin] is established through confession. Repentance is born of confession, and through repentance God is assuaged. Thus *exomologēsis* is a discipline that induces one to prostrate and humble oneself, and enjoins behavior conducive to mercy. Even in matters of dress and food it enjoins the penitent to lie in sackcloth and ashes. It requires covering the body with grungy rags, reducing the soul to lamen-

---

3. Translation from Latin text edited by Philipp Borleffs, *Quinti Septimi Florentis Tertulliani Opera* IV, Corpus Scriptorum Ecclesiasticorum Latinorum, vol. 76 (Vienna: Hoelder-Pichler-Tempsky, 1957), 162–64.

tation, exchanging the committed sins for severe treatment. It mandates knowing only plain food and drink, obviously for the benefit of your spirit rather than your stomach. It commands you to strengthen prayers with fasting, to groan and weep and wail day and night to the Lord your God, to bow before the priests and to kneel before God's beloved, and to adjure all one's brothers and sisters to be an embassy [before God] of one's self-deprecation. *Exomologēsis* enjoins all this in order to render repentance acceptable and to honor the Lord with the fear of punishment, so that it might stand in for God's indignation in pronouncing sentence on the sinner, and by inflicting temporal punishment cancel (I will not say frustrate) the sin's eternal penalty. Therefore by humbling the penitent person, the *exomologēsis* all the more lifts him or her up. By rendering the penitent foul, it all the more purifies him or her. By accusing him, it excuses him. By condemning her, it absolves her. Insofar as you will not have spared yourself—believe me—God will show you his mercy!

10. And yet most people avoid the *exomologēsis* for fear of public exposure and put it off day after day, presumably more concerned with their shame than with their salvation. They are like those who, having contracted a disease in their private body parts, avoid letting their doctors know about it, and thus perish right along with their shame. Certainly it is intolerable for shame itself to be making satisfaction to the Lord when he has been offended, or to be restored to the salvation that has been squandered! Surely you are good for being modest, openly showing your forehead for sin but being bashful for deprecation! I myself have no place for when I gain more at its expense. . . .

1.1.3 Lactantius, *Divine Institutes*, Book 6[4]

24. Let no one quit or be in despair of himself, nevertheless, if, overcome by passion, impelled by lust, deceived by error, or compelled by force, he deviates into the way of unrighteousness. For he can be restored and set free if he repents of his actions and makes satisfaction to God by turning to better ways. Cicero considered this impossible, as he verbalized in his third *Academic*: "But if, as with those who went astray on their journey, it were permissible to repent and correct their error after taking the wrong route, then the emending of their rashness would be easier." But obviously it *is* permissible! For if we perceive that our children repent of their wrongdoing, and judge them to be corrected, and if, in their feeling disinherited and despondent, we pick them up, endear them, and embrace them, why should we despair whether our true Father's clemency can be appeased by our repentance? He who is our Lord and most indulgent Parent promises the remission of sins for those who repent, and the dismissal of all the iniquities of anyone who begins anew in practicing righteousness. For just as the goodness of his past life is of no avail to one who is living in vice now, since his present wickedness nullifies his earlier righteous deeds, so too old sins in no way hinder one who has corrected himself, since his new righteousness wipes away the stain of his earlier life. The one who repents of what he has done understands his former error. Greeks call this *metanoia*, which has a better ring and significance than we can muster with our Latin *resipicentia*. *Resipiscentia* is when one recovers his mind from insanity as it were; he is annoyed with his mistake, and castigates himself for his folly and encourages his soul to better living.... So repentance makes persons cautious and diligent about avoiding sins into which they once fell by being deceived. For no one can be so prudent and circumspect that he does not lapse from time to time; and for this reason God, who knows our feebleness, in his kindness

---

4. Translated from the Latin text edited by Eberhard Heck and Antonie Wlosok, *L. Caelius Firmianus Lactantius Divinarum Institutionum libri septem*, fasc. 3, Bibliotheca Scriptorum Graecorum et Romanorum Teubneriana (Berlin: Walter de Gruyter, 2009), 630–31, 632.

opened a port of salvation, such that the medicine of repentance could relieve of us of the compulsion to which our weakness is subject. So whosoever goes astray, let him retrace his steps and recover and reform himself.

1.2 Repentance as a Lifelong Discipline

1.2.1 John Chrysostom, *Homily* 8 *on Repentance*[5]

Formidable and fearful for the sinner, repentance is a medicine for transgressions, the price of lawlessness, a payment in tears, boldness before God, a weapon against the Devil, a sword cutting off his head, the hope of salvation, the annulment of despair. Repentance opens heaven, introduces us to paradise, overcomes the Devil (which is why I constantly talk about it), just as overconfidence trips us up. Are you a sinner? Do not despair! I do not refrain from applying these medicines, for I realize just how great a weapon your lack of despair is against the Devil. Even if you have sins, do not give up hope. I never stop repeating these things, and if you sin daily, repent daily. Just as we do with old dwellings when they become unsound, we remove what has deteriorated and rebuild them anew, and exercise constant diligence never to neglect them, we do the same in our own lives. If at present you have been worn old by sin, renew yourself with repentance.

1.2.2 Pseudo-Macarius, *Spiritual Homilies*[6]

Homily 4.21

And so, even now, God is good and kind. He shows himself long-suffering toward each one of us. He sees how much each

---

5. Translated from the Greek text in J.-P. Migne, ed., Patrologia Graeca, vol. 49 (Paris: Migne, 1862), col. 337.

6. Translated by George Maloney, *Pseudo-Macarius, The Fifty Spiritual Homilies and the Great Letter*, Classics of Western Spirituality (New York: Paulist Press, 1992), 59–60, 114. Reprinted by permission of Paulist Press.

of us offends him and yet he tranquilly waits until man is converted from sin, and then he is filled with great love and joy. For this is what it means: "There is joy over one sinner that repents" (Luke 15:15), and again, "It is no part of your heavenly Father's plan that a single one of these little ones shall ever come to grief" (Matt 18:14). If anyone, receiving such immense goodness and gentleness of God shown him, would not accept the remission of his every offense, hidden or manifest, while God regards him without a word as he holds out to him repentance, such a person, I say, would be abusing God's kindness by remaining hardened in his sins. In fact, he would add sin to sin. He would join sloth to sloth, heaping one offense upon another. Such a one reaches the limits of his sinning by coming finally to such wickedness that he can no longer extricate himself from its burden....

Homily 15.16–17

Question: Can a man fall who has the gift of grace?

Answer: If he is careless, he certainly falls. For the enemies never take a rest nor do they withdraw from the war. How much more you ought not to cease seeking God! For a very great loss comes to you if you are careless, even though you may seem to be confirmed in the very mystery of grace.

Question: Does grace remain after man's fall?

Answer: God desires to lead man back again to life and to encourage him to weep again and be converted. But if grace truly remains, it is to encourage man again to tears and repentance in order that he may repent because of those things by which he formerly sinned.

1.2.3 Mark the Monk, *On Repentance*[7]

7. I think that the work of repentance is woven together in these three virtues: purging thoughts, praying without ceasing (1 Thess 5:17), and enduring tribulations that come our way—all of which are bound to have effect not only outwardly but spiritually, such that those who endure long-term in them are rendered dispassionate.[8] Since, then, apart from these three virtues the work of repentance cannot be completed, as my discourse has shown, it seems to me that repentance is appropriate to everyone, all the time, both sinners and righteous, if their desire is to be saved. For there is no definition of perfection that does not require the practice of these three named virtues.

For those just starting out, these virtues are an introduction to true piety; for intermediates, they indicate progress; and for the perfect, they provide validation. They are restrained neither by time nor by righteous action but only by bad faith derived from ignorance. This happens when one lapses recklessly into pleasure, using despair as an excuse for hedonism, assuming the teaching of the Novatianists[9] and snubbing repentance. These are the same people who exploit the Apostle when he explains to the Hebrews,[10] who were deliberately sinning and then seeking baptism on a daily basis: "not again laying a foundation of repentance from dead works, and faith in God, and instruction in baptism" (Heb 6:1–2). He said this not because, as these people suggest, he was repudiating repentance—by no means!—but because he was instructing that every function of repentance has

---

7. Translated from the Greek text edited by G.-M. de Durand, *Marc le Moine: Traités* I, Sources Chrétiennes, no. 445 (Paris: Cerf, 1999), 234–38, 246.

8. "Dispassionate" (Greek *apathēs*; noun *apatheia*) is a highly nuanced principle in early Christian asceticism. For some clarification, see the introduction to chapter 7 below.

9. The reference here to Novatianist rigorists from Rome and elsewhere in the third century is a bit awkward. The Novatianists themselves believed that Christians who "lapsed," either under threat of persecution or under the sway of grievous sins, could not be readmitted to the church through repentance. Mark's "pleasure-seekers" here have ostensibly ingested Novatianism simply by presuming that, having already fallen, they are beyond repentance and may as well continue in their hedonism.

10. Numerous early Christian interpreters assumed that Paul had written the epistle to the Hebrews before and even after Origen and others began to cast doubt on Pauline authorship.

a single foundation, the one baptism in Christ, so that those who built their faith on circumcision would not be baptized daily. The Apostle also says, "For it is impossible to renew again to repentance those who have once been enlightened, and who have already tasted the heavenly gift and become partakers in the Holy Spirit, and who have tasted the goodness of the word of God and the powers of the future age, when they have fallen into sin" (Heb 6:4–6). For the Apostle realized that there is only one renewal and foundation proposed for all repentance: holy baptism; so shortly thereafter he adds, "For if we deliberately sin after receiving knowledge of the truth, there no longer remains a sacrifice for sins" (Heb 10:26). . . .

10. But invariably you will ask me, "What need still is there for those who have been truly pleasing to God and who are arriving at perfection to repent?" I concede that there have been and still are such people, but listen and be wise, and you will see how such people need to repent. The Lord says that lying comes from the Devil (John 8:44), and he considered lustful gawking at a woman to be adultery (Matt 5:28). He compared anger toward one's neighbor to murder (Matt 5:21–22), and made clear that one would have to give account of worthless talk. Who is of such character that he is not tempted to lie, who so innocent of ever looking on a woman lustfully, or of ever being furious with a neighbor, or of ever being found responsible for a vain word, that he does not need to repent? Even if there is no such person right now, there was such a person at one time, and he still required repentance until he died. . . .

1.2.4 Augustine, *Sermons* 351 and 352[11]

Sermon 351

2. Now there are three kinds of repentance which, well instructed as you are, you will recognize with me. They are, after all, commonplace in the Church, and known to those who

---

11. Translated by Edmund Hill, *Works of St. Augustine*, vol. 3/10 (Hyde Park, NY: New City Press, 1995), 137–38, 145. Reprinted by permission of New City Press.

attend regularly. One is the sort that is in labor with the new man, until through saving baptism he is cleansed of all past sins; then, as with the birth of a child, the pains that were bringing it to birth are over and done with, and joy follows on anguish....

3. There is a [second] kind of repentance, though, which we should be practicing with the humility of perpetual supplication throughout the whole of this life, which we are spending in the mortal flesh. First of all, because nobody longs for eternal, imperishable and immortal life without repenting of, or regretting, this time-bound, perishable and mortal life. People are not, after all, born into the new life through the sanctification of baptism in such a way that just as they lay aside there all their past sins, they also immediately shed the very mortality of the flesh and its liability to perish. And even if this were not so, there remains the truth of what is written, which all of us also experience in ourselves as long as we are in this life, "that the body which is perishing weighs down the soul, and the earthly habitation depresses the mind thinking many thoughts (Wis 9:15). Because this won't be the case in that state of bliss when "death has been swallowed up in victory" (1 Cor 15:54), who can doubt that whatever kind of temporal well-being we may enjoy, we ought still to be repenting of, or regretting, this life, in order to hasten toward that state of imperishability with all the eagerness we can muster?

That's also the drift, you see, of what the apostle says: "As long as we are in the body, we are traveling abroad from the Lord; for we are walking by faith, not be sight" (2 Cor 5:6–7). So who will be in a hurry and a lather to return to the home country, and to contemplate that sight face to face, unless they regret and are sorry for their exile abroad?...

Sermon 352

7. And so we are reminded to talk now about a second kind of repentance. I suggested, you remember, that it is considered in scripture under three headings. There is the first kind for the *competentes* and those thirsting to come to baptism; this I have

illustrated from the holy scriptures. Well, there's another sort of repentance for every day. And where can I show you this daily repentance? I have no better place to show it in than in the daily prayer, in which the Lord taught us to pray, showed us what we should say to the Father, and put the matter in these words: Forgive us our debts, just as we too forgive our debtors" (Matt 6:12). What debts, brothers and sisters? Since debts here can only be understood as sins, are we praying for the debts that he canceled in baptism to be canceled over again? Undoubtedly every single Egyptian who was pursuing us is dead. If there's nothing left over from the enemies who were pursuing us, what are we praying to have forgiven, if not the drooping of our arms against Amalek? "Forgive us, just as we forgive." He provided a medicine, he sealed a bargain. First he dictates a prayer, next he replies to you praying. He knows what rules govern the way things are done in heaven, and how you can obtain the things you desire. "Do you want to be forgiven? Forgive," he says....

1.3 Repentance as Compunction

1.3.1 *Sayings of the Desert Fathers (Alphabetical Collection)*[12]

Arsenius, ch. 41: It was said of him that he had a hollow in his chest channeled out by the tears which fell from his eyes all his life while he sat at his manual work. When Abba Poemen learned that he was dead, he said weeping, "Truly you are blessed, Abba Arsenius, for you wept for yourself in this world! He who does not weep for himself here below will weep eternally hereafter; so it is impossible not to weep, either voluntarily or when compelled through suffering."

Matoes, ch. 12: A brother said to Abba Matoes, "Give me a word." He said to him, "Restrain the spirit of controversy in yourself in everything and weep, have compunction, for the time is drawing near."

---

12. Translated by Benedicta Ward (Collegeville, MN: Liturgical Press/Cistercian Publications, 1975), 18, 145, 173, 195. Used by permission of Liturgical Press. All rights reserved.

Poemen, ch. 50: A brother asked Abba Poemen, "What should I do?" The old man said to him, "When Abraham entered the promised land he bought a sepulchre for himself and by means of this tomb, he inherited the land." The brother said to him, "What is the tomb?" The old man said, "The place of tears and compunction."

Poemen, ch. 208: A brother asked Abba Poemen, "What can I do about my sins?" and the old man said to him, "Weep interiorly, for both deliverance from faults and the acquisition of virtues are gained through compunction."

Poemen, ch. 209: He also said, "Weeping is the way that Scripture and our Fathers have handed on to us."

1.3.2 Evagrius of Pontus, *On Prayer*[13]

5. First of all, pray to receive the gift of tears, in order that through compunction you may settle the unruliness that infests your soul, and then, having confessed against yourself your lawlessness to the Lord (Ps 31:5), you may acquire his forgiveness.

6. Use tears to gain the fulfilment of your every request, for the Lord rejoices exceedingly over you when he receives a prayer drenched with tears.

7. Even if you cry fountains of tears when you pray, by no means let yourself be puffed up as though you were superior to many others. For your prayer had help to enable you to confess your sins and be reconciled with the Lord through your tears.

8. So do not turn the remedy for the passions into a passion itself, lest you further anger the very one who has bestowed grace. Many who weep for their sins have forgotten the purpose of their tears, and in their madness they have gone astray.

---

13. Translated from the Greek text in J.-P. Migne, ed., Patrologia Graeca, vol. 79 (Paris: J.-P. Migne, 1865), cols. 1168D–1169B. (This work of Evagrius comes down to us under an erroneous ascription to Nilus of Ancyra.)

1.3.3 John Cassian, *Conference* 9[14]

29. Abba Isaac: "Not every profusion of tears is induced by the same feeling or virtue. For one form of weeping originates from the thorns of our sins piercing our heart, of which is it said: 'I have labored in my lamentation. Every night I will wash my bed, and water my couch with tears' (Ps 6:6). And elsewhere: 'Let your tears run down like a torrent day and night; give yourself no rest, and do not let the apple of your eye be quiet' (Lam 2:18).

"Weeping arises in a different way from the contemplation of eternal benefits and the desire for that future splendor which, in its own right, prompts even fuller fountains of tears of irrepressible joy and boundless exultation as our soul thirsts for the mighty and living God, saying, 'When will I come and appear in the presence of God? My tears have been my bread day and night' (Ps 42:2–3). With daily wailing and lamentation, our soul declares, 'Woe is me that my sojourning is prolonged,' and 'Too long has my soul been a sojourner' (Ps 120:5–6).

"There is still another reason that tears flow, which is not on account of any consciousness of mortal sin, but because of a fear of Gehenna and the recollection of that terrible judgment about which the prophet, himself stricken with terror, prays to God saying, 'Do not enter into judgment with your servant, for in your sight no living person shall be justified' (Ps 143:2). There is even another kind of tears, generated not by consciousness of oneself but by the obduracy and sins of others. Samuel wept for Saul with these tears, as did both the Lord in the Gospel (cf. Luke 19:41), and long before Jeremiah, over Jerusalem. As Jeremiah said, 'Who will give water for my head, and a fountain of tears for my eyes? Day and night I will lament the slain of the daughter of my people' (Jer 9:1). Undoubtedly these are the sort of tears of which Psalm 101 sings: 'I have eaten ashes as my bread, and mixed my cup with weeping' (Ps 101:9 Vulgate; Ps 102:9 Hebrew). These are certainly not tears arising from the

---

14. Translated from the Latin text edited by Michael Petschenig, *Ioannis Cassianis Opera* II, Corpus Scriptorum Ecclesiasticorum Latinorum, vol. 13 (Vienna: Geroldi, 1886), 274–76.

same feeling as in Psalm 6, where tears emerge from the person of the penitent, but were due rather to the anxieties, difficulties, and hardships of this life that oppress the righteous in this world. This is made evident to us not only by the text of Psalm 101 but its title: 'A prayer of the poor man when he was in distress and poured forth his prayer to God' (Ps 101:1 Vulgate; Ps 102:1 Hebrew). This is none other than the poor person mentioned in the Gospel: 'Blessed are the poor in spirit, for theirs is the kingdom of heaven' (Matt 5:3).

30. "Hence there is a vast difference between these tears and those that are squeezed from the parched eyes of one who is still hard of heart. It is not that we believe that the latter are entirely fruitless—for the attempt to shed them is for a good purpose, especially for those who have not yet been able to arrive at perfect knowledge, or be thoroughly cleansed from their past or present vices. But one who has already arrived at a virtuous state of mind has no business forcing a profusion of tears in this way or attempting with great effort to shed the tears of the outer man. Even if they have been produced one way or the other, they will never match the richness of spontaneous tears. For those who pray attempting that kind of weeping tend more to degrade their minds, to humiliate them, to plunge them into human concerns and resign them from that heavenly sublimity where the astounded mind of the one who prays must be irremovably fixed; they will instead force the mind, once it has relaxed the intensity of its prayers, to become weak from sterile, fabricated, and paltry tears."

1.3.4 Jacob of Sarug, *Homily on the Sinful Woman*[15]

Oh woman,[16] full of blemishes, you whose beauties are many!
I am so amazed at you, and how I shall describe you I do not know.

---

15. Translated by Scott Fitzgerald Johnson, *Jacob of Sarug's Homily on the Sinful Woman*, Texts from Christian Late Antiquity 33 (Piscataway, NJ: Gorgias, 2013), 30–32, 68–70, 80. Reprinted by permission of Gorgias Press. Jacob's format here is the Syriac *memre*, or homily in verse.
16. Luke 7:36–50.

Happy mother, who conceived iniquity and gave birth to deceit,
But who in forgiveness gained purity and holiness.

Lover of falsehood, who passed many years in it,
But whose effect is magnified, just as the apostles in their preaching.

Mistress of sins, who was polluted by her own deeds,
Jesus with his hyssop purified and cleansed her, and she became pure (Ps 51:7).

Putrid spring, out of whom sprung every kind of evil,
But mercy converted her, and streams which were bitter became sweet (Exod 15:25).

Troubled of soul, who had become dark through her offenses,
Jesus the Light shined and made lucid her gloominess (John 1:5; 8:12; 9:5).

A vulture, who snatched up shamelessly everyone who met her,
Christ the Eagle made her a dove after she saw Him.

A stone, which was a stumbling block of iniquity for everyone who came to her,
But behold! She was set upon the foundation of apostleship (Matt 16:18).

A she-wolf, who approached the Chief Shepherd,
But after she saw Him she became a ewe in His field.

A woman, who transgressed through many evil deeds,
Sings lovingly her own name as gospel.

Hater of life whom iniquity covered most of her days,
But Christ adorned her to become a princess of the beautiful things.

All of creation was represented in the defiled woman,
Who through the advent of Jesus became beautiful and pure.

In the oil and tears that she poured out there on the Savior,
She prefigured the baptism of the world for the world symbolically. . . .

Oil and tears she poured out there upon the Holy One,
With the result that the entire ritual of baptism was completed.

The excellent oil and the little water were mixed.
The Great High Priest made atonement for the defiled girl by performing His own part (Heb 4:4–10:31).

The wise woman knelt before the Forgiver,
In order to come to spiritual birth, which she lacked.

She bent her head over to wipe His feet with her hair (Luke 7:38; John 12:3)
And just as in baptism she received holiness from the Holy One.

She entered into the second womb, the place of atonement (John 3:4). . . .

Not even today is His treasury lacking in forgiveness.
It is full just as it has always been, and its door will be opened for the one who seeks Him.

Whoever has pains in his body should run unto Him.
And whoever iniquity of the soul has marked should take shelter in Him.

Bring tears, just like the prostitute, to the house of God.
And receive, just like her, forgiveness of sins for yourselves. . . .

1.4 The Ecclesial Dimension of Repentance

1.4.1 Ambrose of Milan, *On Repentance*, Book 2[17]

2.10.91. Can anyone endure that you should blush to entreat God, when you do not blush to entreat a fellow human being? That you should be ashamed to entreat him who knows you fully, when you are not ashamed to confess your sins to another person who knows you not? Do you shrink from witnesses and sympathizers in your prayers, when, if you have to satisfy one person, you must visit many and entreat them to be kind enough to intervene; when you throw yourself at someone's knees, kiss his or her feet, bring your children, still unconscious of guilt, also to plead for their father's pardon? And you disdain to do this in the Church in order to entreat God, in order to gain for yourself the support of the holy congregation; where there is no cause for shame, except indeed not to confess, since we are all sinners, amongst whom that person is the most praiseworthy who is the most humble; that one is the most righteous who feels himself or herself the lowest.

2.10.92. Let the Church, our Mother, weep for you, and wash away your guilt with her tears; let Christ see you mourning and say, "Blessed are ye that are sad, for ye shall rejoice" (Luke 6:21). It pleases him that many should entreat for one. In the Gospel, too, moved by the widow's tears, because many were weeping for her, he raised her son (Luke 7:11–17). He heard Peter more quickly when he raised Dorcas, because the poor were mourning over the death of the woman (Acts 9:36–42). He also forthwith forgave Peter, for he wept most bitterly (Luke 22:62). And if you weep bitterly Christ will look upon you and your guilt shall leave you. For the application of pain does away with the enjoyment of the wickedness and the delight of the sin. And so while mourning over our past sins we shut the door against fresh

---

17. Translated by H. de Romestin, E. de Romestin, and H. T. F. Duckworth, *Some of the Principal Works of St. Ambrose*, Nicene and Post-Nicene Fathers, 2nd series, vol. 10 (Edinburgh: T&T Clark, 1896). Revised and updated.

ones, and from the condemnation of our guilt there arises as it were a training in innocence.

2.10.93. Let, then, nothing call you away from penitence, for this you have in common with the saints, and would that such sorrowing for sin as that of the saints were copied by you. David, as it were, "ate ashes for bread, and mingled his drink with tears" (Ps 102:9), and therefore now rejoices the more because he wept the more: "Mine eyes ran down," he said, "with rivers of water" (Ps 119:136).

2.10.94. John wept much (Rev 5:4), and, as he tells us, the mysteries of Christ were revealed to him. But that woman who, when she was in sin and ought to have wept, nevertheless rejoiced, and covered herself with a robe of purple and scarlet (Rev 17:4), and adorned herself with much gold and precious stones, now mourns the misery of eternal weeping.

2.10.95. Deservedly are they blamed who think that they often do penance, for they are licentious toward Christ. For if they went through their penance in truth, they would not think that it could be repeated again; for as there is but one baptism, so there is but one course of penance, so far as the outward practice goes, for we must repent of our daily faults, but this latter has to do with lighter faults, the former with such as are graver.

2.10.96. But I have more easily found such ones as had preserved their innocence than such as had fittingly repented. Does anyone think that that is penitence where there still exists the striving after earthly honors, where wine flows, and even conjugal relations take place? The world must be renounced; less sleep must be indulged in than nature demands; it must be broken by groans, interrupted by sighs, put aside by prayers; the mode of life must be such that we die to the usual habits of life. Let one deny oneself and be wholly changed, as in the fable they relate of a certain youth, who left his home because of his love for a harlot, and, having subdued his love, returned; then one day meeting his old favorite and not speaking to her, she, being surprised and supposing that he had not recognized her, said, when they met again, "It is I." "But," he answered, "I am not the former I."

1.4.2 Caesarius of Arles, *Sermon* 67[18]

Whenever we see some of our brothers or sisters perform public penance, by God's inspiration, dearly beloved, we can and should stir up great compunction in our hearts. Who would not rejoice and be glad, giving thanks to God to the best of his or her ability, when seeing sinners angry over their sins and proclaiming this in a loud voice? Indeed, what those sinners formerly defended with great insolence they now begin to blame in a salutary manner. Such sinners have now begun to be united with God, because they no longer want to defend their sins, but to punish them. Moreover, since God detests sin, as soon as sinners begin to hate it also by despising and turning aside from their faults they are united to God. As a matter of fact, those who do public penance could have performed it privately. However, after considering the multitude of their sins, they feel that they are not strong enough to oppose their great vices alone, and so they want to solicit the assistance of all the people. In like manner, when a vineyard has become barren through neglect, a man invites his neighbors and friends, and on a certain day the whole crowd assembles to repair the damage, because with the help of many hands what cannot be repaired by one is accomplished. For this reason a person who wants to perform public penance, assembles a congregation, as it were, so that, aided by the prayers of all the people, that person may be able to tear out the thorns and briers of his or her sins. Thus, with God's help, a harvest of virtue may be able to spring up, so that the vineyard of the penitent's heart which had been accustomed to grow thorns, not grapes, may begin to produce the sweetness of spiritual wine. Nor should we regard with indifference the fact that the penitent is covered with a hair shirt. Because the hair shirt is made

---

18. Translated by Mary Magdeleine Mueller, *St. Caesarius of Arles: Sermons* I, Fathers of the Church, vol. 31 (Washington, DC: Catholic University of America Press, 1956), 318–19, 320. Reprinted by permission of the Catholic University of America Press.

of goat's hair and goats represent sin, the penitent publicly confesses to being not a lamb but a goat. By these signs the penitent proclaims aloud: Look at me, everyone, and shed pious tears for me in my misery....

I speak the truth, brothers and sisters, when I say that one must be thought wicked and inhuman if not sympathizing with one who seeks repentance in this manner.... Therefore, what we wish to receive from others if we are disposed to do public penance we should hasten to do for others with our whole heart and soul. What did we want when we deserved to seek the remedy of repentance, except that everyone should endeavor to implore divine mercy for us? For this reason, we should with perfect charity confer upon others what we desire to receive from them, according to the words: "Confess your sins to one another, and pray for one another, that you may be saved" (James 5:16), and "a brother helping his brother shall be exalted" (Prov 18:19).

2.

Resisting Worldly Powers and Renouncing Worldly Evils

INTRODUCTION

The relation of emergent Christianity to the Roman Empire and to Roman culture is far more complex than the simplistic portrait of a hunted sect, constantly fighting for its life until the end of the persecutions, will allow. Taken altogether, Christian apologists and polemicists of the second and third centuries reveal, broadly speaking, a dialectic of resistance and accommodation, and one that did not abruptly end with Constantine's amnesty. Obviously the ethos of resistance was most pronounced and rhetorically amplified in those times and places where public excoriation of Christianity was most intense and the threat or reality of persecution most severe. But "in between" those times and places certain Christian apologists proactively sought to negotiate and rationalize Christianity's presence in the Roman Empire.[1]

Resistance, after all, could assume different forms. One form was a passive resistance that maintained Christianity's intrinsic difference from the cultural and religious status quo, with no

---

1. An excellent example here is the *Plea (Legatio) on Behalf of Christians* of the second-century apologist Athenagoras of Athens.

insinuation of rebelliousness. Already in the New Testament, the Johannine literature and Paul spoke negatively of human culture as "the world" or "this age" (cf. John 15:18–19; 1 John 2:15–17; 1 Cor 2:6, 8; 2 Cor 4:4; Gal 4:3) tragically alienated from God and hostile to the gospel, leaving Christians resident aliens from the outset.[2] But this argument could take a more conciliatory tone, as in the unknown second-century writer of the *Epistle to Diognetus* [2.1], whose memorable line about Christians being "in but not of the world" has been quoted countless times. The author presses an argument often found in other apologists of the time. Even if their religion is an affront to pagan idolatry, and they remain resident aliens of a sort, Christians are a healthy moral leaven in the world, and by their peaceable and godly ways they uphold rather than undermine the peace and stability. As Origen says in much the same spirit as the *Epistle to Diognetus*, Christians are an ameliorating "army of piety" even if they resist formal public service in the empire.[3]

But from the North African churches, which were especially devastated by persecution, came a literature of ardent protest and open defiance, exemplified most famously in the diatribes of the Christian lawyer Tertullian (ca. 155–ca. 240). In several writings, including the *Letter to the Martyrs* excerpted here [2.2], Tertullian set an aggressive and apocalyptic tone in describing Christianity's foreignness on earth. In the *Letter*, he suggests that the imprisoned martyrs-to-be are actually fortunate—their prison being the "devil's house" but paradoxically also a halfway house to heaven preparing them to transcend the world once for all—while other Christians remain behind as hostages of paganism. Tertullian counseled Christians not to shrink from resisting an empire bent on moral self-destruction, using their scrupulously disciplined lifestyle as a weapon. This apocalyptic tone continued in Cyprian (200–258), bishop of Carthage during the severe general persecution instigated by the Emperor Decius in 250. His letter to the beleaguered Christians in Thibaris [2.3] encourages endurance in the face of profound suffering as a consummate *imitatio Christi* and as a sure path to final vindication.

2. See Meeks, *Origins of Christian Morality*, 52–65.
3. *Against Celsus* 8.73.

Resistance as Christian social protest against the empire did occur, even if at times indirectly. It was manifest in positions taken against Christian participation in civil service and the military, in the open defiance of Roman entertainment culture, and more. But this kind of resistance did not end with the arrival of Constantine. The naive perception that the church suddenly and blithely embraced a new "imperial" status is flatly wrong, although that story is too substantial to analyze here. I have provided a brief sample of post-Constantinian Christian protest in the virulent condemnation of the Roman slavery system leveled by the Cappadocian bishop Gregory of Nyssa [2.4] in the fourth century. Though it is not typical of all episcopal sentiments in this period (John Chrysostom, for example, promotes Christian reconciliation between masters and slaves rather than immediate abolition of slavery), Gregory's rebuke of the social order provided an important precedent. The Cappadocian Fathers and other bishops and leaders stood their ground in numerous instances not only against the neo-pagan Emperor Julian "the Apostate" (r. 360–363) but against Christian emperors alleged to be incompetent or overly meddlesome in the church's affairs. Numerous leaders and thinkers never really embraced the Christianized doctrine of the divine right of kings originally espoused by Eusebius of Caesarea on behalf of Constantine.

While the thesis that monasticism was purely a moral protest against the imperial establishment of the church in the fourth and fifth centuries has rightly been overturned, there is no question that monastic theologians carried forward a prophetic tradition that targeted "worldly" seductions and marked moral boundaries of which all Christians were to take notice. The early Byzantine sage John Climacus (ca. 579–ca. 649), a monk of Mt. Sinai, epitomized the need for monks and ascetics to forsake the relentless trappings of the secular domain, including family [2.5]. Renunciation was intrinsic to radical discipleship—a message that applied, by extension, even to non-monastics who would never undertake the full "exile" (*xeniteia*) from the world that Climacus demanded of monks.

THE TEXTS

2.1 *Epistle to Diognetus*[4]

5. For the Christians are distinguished from other people neither by country, nor language, nor the customs which they observe. For they neither inhabit cities of their own, nor employ a peculiar form of speech, nor lead a life which is marked out by any singularity. The teaching which they follow has not been devised by any speculation or deliberation of the inquisitive; nor do they, like some, proclaim themselves the advocates of any merely human doctrines. But, inhabiting Greek as well as barbarian cities, according as the lot of each of them has determined, and following the customs of the natives in respect to clothing, food, and the rest of their ordinary conduct, they display to us their wonderful and confessedly striking method of life. They dwell in their own countries, but simply as sojourners. As citizens, they share in all things with others, and yet endure all things as if foreigners. Every foreign land is to them as their native country, and every land of their birth as a land of strangers. They marry, as do all [others]; they beget children; but they do not destroy their offspring. They have a common table, but not a common bed. They are in the flesh, but they do not live after the flesh. They pass their days on earth, but they are citizens of heaven. They obey the prescribed laws, and at the same time surpass the laws by their lives. They love all men, and are persecuted by all. They are unknown and condemned; they are put to death, and restored to life. They are poor, yet make many rich; they are in lack of all things, and yet abound in all; they are dishonored, and yet in their very dishonor are glorified. They are evil spoken of, and yet are justified; they are reviled, and bless; they are insulted, and repay the insult with honor; they do good, yet are punished as evil-doers. When punished, they rejoice as if enlivened; they are assailed by the Jews as foreigners,

---

4. Translated by Alexander Roberts and James Donaldson, *The Apostolic Fathers, with Justin Martyr and Irenaeus,* Ante-Nicene Fathers, vol. 1 (Edinburgh: T&T Clark, 1885), 26–27. Revised and updated.

and are persecuted by the Greeks; yet those who hate them are unable to assign any reason for their hatred.

6. To sum up—what the soul is in the body, that is what Christians are in the world. The soul is dispersed through all the members of the body, and Christians are scattered through all the cities of the world. The soul dwells in the body, yet is not of the body; and Christians dwell in the world, yet are not of the world. The invisible soul is guarded by the visible body, and Christians are known indeed to be in the world, but their godliness remains invisible. The flesh hates the soul, and wars against it, though itself suffering no injury, because it is prevented from enjoying pleasures; the world also hates the Christians, though in nowise injured, because they abjure pleasures. The soul loves the flesh that hates it, and [loves also] the members; Christians likewise love those that hate them. The soul is imprisoned in the body, yet preserves that very body; and Christians are confined in the world as in a prison, and yet they are the preservers of the world. The immortal soul dwells in a mortal tabernacle; and Christians dwell as sojourners in corruptible [bodies], looking for an incorruptible dwelling in the heavens. The soul, when but ill-provided with food and drink, becomes better; in like manner, the Christians, though subjected day by day to punishment, increase the more in number. God has assigned them this illustrious position, which it were unlawful for them to forsake.

2.2 Tertullian, *Letter to the Martyrs*[5]

1. Mark, blessed martyrs: Along with the provision which our lady mother the Church from her bountiful breasts, and each brother or sister out of his or her private means, makes for your bodily wants in the prison, accept also from me some contribution to your spiritual sustenance; for it is not good that the flesh be feasted and the spirit starve: on the contrary, if that which is weak be carefully looked to, it is but right that that which is still weaker should not be neglected. Not that I am specially entitled

---

5. Translated by Sydney Thelwall, *Latin Christianity: Its Founder, Tertullian*, Ante-Nicene Fathers, vol. 3 (Edinburgh: T&T Clark, 1885), 693, 694. Revised and updated.

to exhort you; yet not only the trainers and overseers, but even the unskilled, nay, all who choose, without the slightest need for it, are wont to animate from afar by their cries the most accomplished gladiators, and from the mere throng of onlookers useful suggestions have sometimes come; first, then, O blessed, grieve not the Holy Spirit (Eph 4:30) who has entered the prison with you; for if he had not gone with you there, you would not have been there this day. Give all endeavor, therefore, to retain him; so let him lead you thence to your Lord. The prison, indeed, is the Devil's house as well, wherein he keeps his family. But you have come within its walls for the very purpose of trampling the Wicked One under foot in his chosen abode. You had already in pitched battle outside utterly overcome him. . . .

2. Other things, hindrances equally of the soul, may have accompanied you as far as the prison gate, to which also your relatives may have attended you. There and thenceforth you were severed from the world; how much more from the ordinary course of worldly life and all its affairs! Nor let this separation from the world alarm you; for if we reflect that the world is more really the prison, we shall see that you have gone out of a prison rather than into one. The world has the greater darkness, blinding persons' hearts. The world imposes the more grievous fetters, binding persons' very souls. The world breathes out the worst impurities—human lusts. The world contains the larger number of criminals, even the whole human race. Then, last of all, it awaits the judgment, not of the proconsul, but of God. Wherefore, O blessed, you may regard yourselves as having been translated from a prison to, we may say, a place of safety. It is full of darkness, but you yourselves are light; it has bonds, but God has made you free. . . .

3. Grant now, O blessed, that even to Christians the prison is unpleasant; yet we were called to the warfare of the living God in our very response to the sacramental [baptismal] words. Well, no soldier comes out to the campaign laden with luxuries, nor does he go to action from his comfortable chamber, but from the light and narrow tent, where every kind of hardness, roughness and unpleasantness must be put up with. Even in peace soldiers

inure themselves to war by toils and inconveniences—marching in arms, running over the plain, working at the ditch, making the *testudo*, engaging in many arduous labors. The sweat of the brow is on everything, that bodies and minds may not shrink at having to pass from shade to sunshine, from sunshine to icy cold, from the robe of peace to the coat of mail, from silence to clamor, from quiet to tumult. In like manner, O blessed ones, count whatever is hard in this lot of yours as a discipline of your powers of mind and body. You are about to pass through a noble struggle, in which the living God acts the part of superintendent, in which the Holy Spirit is your trainer, in which the prize is an eternal crown of angelic dignity, citizenship in the heavens, glory everlasting.

2.3 Cyprian of Carthage, *Letter* 58 (*To the People of Thibaris*)[6]

1. You ought to know and to believe, and hold it for certain, that the day of affliction has begun to hang over our heads, and the end of the world and the time of Antichrist to draw near, so that we must all stand prepared for the battle; nor consider anything but the glory of life eternal, and the crown of the confession of the Lord; and not regard those things which are coming as being such as were those which have passed away. A severer and a fiercer fight is now threatening, for which the soldiers of Christ ought to prepare themselves with uncorrupted faith and robust courage, considering that they drink the cup of Christ's blood daily, for the reason that they themselves also may be able to shed their blood for Christ. For this is to wish to be found with Christ, to imitate that which Christ both taught and did, according to the Apostle John, who said, "He who says that he abides in Christ ought to walk even as he walked" (1 John 2:6). Moreover, the blessed Apostle Paul exhorts and teaches, saying, "We are God's children; but if children, then heirs of God, and joint-heirs with Christ, provided that we suffer with him, that we may also be glorified with him" (Rom 8:16–17). . . .

---

6. Translated by Ernest Wallis, *Hippolytus, Cyprian, Caius, Novatian*, Ante-Nicene Fathers, vol. 5 (Edinburgh: T&T Clark, 1885), 347, 349–50. Revised and updated.

2. Nor let any one of you, beloved brothers and sisters, be so terrified by the fear of future persecution, or the coming of the threatening Antichrist, as not to be found armed for all things by the Gospel's exhortations and precepts, and by the heavenly warnings. Antichrist is coming, but above him comes Christ also. The Enemy goes about and rages, but immediately the Lord follows to avenge our sufferings and our wounds. The Adversary is enraged and threatens, but there is one who can deliver us from his hands. He is to be feared whose anger no one can escape, as he himself forewarns, and says: "Fear not them who kill the body, but are not able to kill the soul; but rather fear him who is able to destroy both body and soul in hell" (Matt 10:28). And again: "Whoever loves his life shall lose it; and whoever that hates his life in this world shall keep it unto life eternal" (John 12:25). And in Revelation the Lord instructs and forewarns, saying, "If any one worships the beast and his image, and receive his mark in his forehead or in his hand, the same also shall drink of the wine of the wrath of God, mixed in the cup of his indignation, and he shall be tormented with fire and brimstone in the presence of the holy angels, and in the presence of the Lamb; and the smoke of their torments shall ascend up for ever and ever; and they shall have no rest day or night who worship the beast and his image" (Rev 14:9–11).

3. For the secular contest men are trained and prepared, and reckon it a great glory of their honor if it should happen to them to be crowned in the sight of the people, and in the presence of the emperor. Behold a lofty and great contest, glorious also with the reward of a heavenly crown, inasmuch as God looks upon us as we struggle, and, extending his view over those whom he has condescended to make his sons, he enjoys the spectacle of our contest. God looks upon us in the warfare, and fighting in the encounter of faith; his angels look on us, and Christ looks on us. How great is the dignity, and how great the happiness of the glory, to engage in the presence of God, and to be crowned, with Christ for a judge! Let us be armed, beloved brothers and sisters, with our whole strength, and let us be prepared for the struggle with an uncorrupted mind, with a sound faith, with a devoted courage....

2.4 Gregory of Nyssa, *Homily 4 on Ecclesiastes*[7]

"I procured slaves and slave-girls," he says, "and homebred slaves were born for me" (Eccl 2:7). Do you see the magnitude of his bragging here? Such talk exalts itself in an open affront to God.[8] For we hear from prophecy that "all things universally are slaves" of the Authority who transcends all things (Ps 119:91). Thus when a man makes one of God's possessions his own possession, he imparts dominion to his own human kind, simultaneously supposing himself the master of men and women. What is he doing but arrogantly pressing beyond his own nature, viewing himself as above and beyond those whom he rules?

"I procured slaves and slave-girls." What are you saying? You condemn to slavery fellow human beings whose very nature is free and endowed with self-determination! You legislate directly against God, and subvert his law regarding human nature! Under the yoke of slavery you subjugate the very one who was created precisely for the purpose of being master of the earth, appointed by the Creator to rule it, and in so doing you defy and controvert God's own command. You forget the limits of your own authority, because your rule is confined only to control of irrational creatures. For Scripture says, "Let them rule" over birds, fishes, four-footed animals and those that creep on the ground (Gen 1:26). How is it that you exceed the scope of your own domain and raise yourself up against human nature when it is free, numbering human beings right along with four-footed animals or even animals without feet? The word of prophecy cries out "You have subjected all things" to humanity, and enumerating the things made subject, it includes "oxen," "cattle," and "sheep" (Ps 8:7–8). Have human beings been born of oxen in your view? Do cattle produce human offspring, so far as you are concerned? Irrational animals alone are the slaves of human beings. But for you they are insufficient? Scripture speaks [of the

---

7. Translated from the Greek text edited by James McDonough and Paul Alexander, *In Inscriptiones Psalmorum; In Sextum Psalmum; In Ecclesiasten Homiliae,* Gregorii Nysseni Opera, vol. 5 (Leiden: Brill, 1962), 334–38.

8. In this and his other homilies on Ecclesiastes, Gregory understands Solomon to be the author of the more profane confessions in the text, while Christ, the true Ecclesiast, authors its spiritually fertile insights.

Lord] "raising up grass for the cattle and plants for the service of human beings" (Ps 104:14). But by dividing human nature between those who are slaves and those who are masters, you cause it to be enslaved to itself and mastered by itself.

"I procured slaves and slave-girls." Tell me, for what price? What did you find that was as valuable as human nature itself? What kind of value do you place on reason? How many obols do you consider of equal value to the image of God? How many silver coins did you give up for human nature that was formed by God? God said, "Let us make humanity in our image and likeness" (Gen 1:26). Given that humanity is created in God's likeness, rules over all the earth, and has been invested by God with authority over all earthly things, tell me, who is its seller? Who is its buyer? Only God has this power, or rather not even God himself. "For his gifts," says Scripture, are "irrevocable" (Rom 11:29). God, then, would not reduce human nature to slavery, since he recalled us, who were deliberately enslaved to sin, to freedom. But if God does not enslave what is free, who is it that positions his own dominion over God's? And how shall the human being, who rules over all the earth and all earthly things, be put up for sale? For all the belongings and property of persons being sold are sold along with them. So how much do we consider all the earth to be worth? How much everything existing on the earth? If these things are priceless, what price, tell me, is worthy of the one who is over them? Were you to say "the whole world," you still would not have thereby found the price which that ruler is worth. For he who perfectly knows human nature said that the cosmos itself could not be a worthy exchange for the human soul (cf. Matt 16:26). So whenever a human being is up for sale, it is none other than the ruler of the earth who is being led to auction; and so clearly his or her current property is also put up for auction—which would include land, islands, sea, and all that is in them. What, then, shall the buyer pay, and what will the seller take in return, given how much property is being transacted in the deal?

But has the little invoice, the written contract, and the counting up of the obols deceived you into thinking you are sovereign over the "image of God"? How foolish you are! Were the contract lost, its written terms eaten up by worms, or a drop of water to stain and ruin it, what would you have to prove their enslavement? What provision would you have for your ownership? I see nothing else to vouch for your superiority over your subordinates but the mere title of owner. What does this authority add to your human nature? Neither longevity, nor beauty, nor good health, nor superiority in virtue. You descend from the same ancestors. You have the same kind of life. The same passions of soul and body prevail over both you the master and the one yoked under your mastery: the same pains and satisfactions, the same joys and troubles, the same griefs and pleasures, the same angers and fears, and the same diseases and death. What difference is there in any of these things between slave and master? Do they not draw in the same air when they breathe? Do they not see the sun in the same way? Do they not alike find natural sustenance by consuming food? Do they not have the very same anatomical structure? Do the two not become one common dust after they die? Will they not see one and the same judgment, a common kingdom and a common Gehenna? Being equal, therefore, in all these things, in what way do you have more privilege, tell me, such that, as a human being, you consider yourself the master of other human beings, saying, "I procured slaves and slave-girls," as if they were goats and pigs? For when the Preacher said, "I procured slaves and slave-girls," he added that an abundance of flocks of sheep and cattle herds accrued to him. For he says, "much property in flocks of sheep and cattle herds came to me" (Eccl 2:7b), as if claiming that these animals and human slaves were equally under his authority. . . .

2.5 John Climacus, *The Ladder of Divine Ascent*[9]

Step 1: On Renunciation of Life

Let the one who leaves the world in order to throw off the burden of his sins imitate those who sit in front of tombs outside the city. Let him not cease from his intense and fervent tears, nor from the silent cries of his heart, until he sees Jesus himself

---

9. Translated from the Greek text in J.-P. Migne, ed., *Patrologia Graeca*, vol. 88 (Paris: J.-P. Migne, 1864), cols. 633D–636B, 656D–657C, 664B–C, 664D.

coming to roll away the stone of feverishness from his heart, to deliver his mind—this Lazarus of ours!—from the chains of sin, exhorting his ministering angels, "Release him from his passions and allow him to proceed toward blessed dispassion." Unless the renunciation takes this shape, there is no benefit. Those of us [monks] who desire to flee Egypt and escape Pharaoh invariably require a Moses to be our mediator with God, standing on our behalf between ascetic practice and contemplation[10] with his hands outstretched before the Lord, so that, under his guidance, we may pass through the sea of sins and turn back the Amalek of the passions (cf. Exod 17:11–13). Those who have devoted themselves to God but suppose that they need no leader are deceiving themselves. The refugees from Egypt had Moses as their leader. Those fleeing Sodom had an angel. The former resemble those who cure the passions of the soul through the diligent care of doctors; these are the refugees from Egypt. The escapees from Sodom, on the other hand, are those who strongly desire to divest the wretched body of its corruption, wherefore they demand to be aided, as I said, by an angel or angelic equivalent. We ourselves require someone exceedingly skilled, a doctor, for our gangrenous wounds. Those aspiring to ascend to heaven with the body must invariably endure violence (cf. Matt 11:12) and relentless pain. This is especially true for those who are in the early stages of renunciation, at which point our habit for pleasure-seeking and our callous heart must be put through blatant suffering en route to the love of God and purity. . . .

Step 2: On Detachment

Mortifying the belly, standing up all night long, drinking a small ration of water, denying yourself bread, the purifying cup of dishonor—all these show you the narrow way. So will being scorned, ridiculed, jeered—things proper to cutting off

10. The ancient philosophical tandem of "practice" (*praxis*) and "contemplation" (*theōria*), discussed briefly in my general introduction, was taken over into early Christian ethics to describe the two principal disciplines of growth in Christ. Especially (though not exclusively) in monastic settings, "practice" evoked the active life of self-renunciation and positive performance of Christ's commandments, and "contemplation" the quest for spiritual insight into God's reality as revealed through created nature, Scripture, and mystical theological experience.

self-will—enduring opposition, not complaining about neglect, putting up with fierce insolence, being strong to endure injustice, not being angered in the face of others' contempt, remaining humble in the face of condemnation. Blessed are those who follow the way of the aforesaid disciplines, for theirs is the kingdom of heaven.

Nobody can enter the heavenly bridal chamber with a crown without first undertaking the first, second, and third renunciations. First he must renounce worldly matters, human attachments, and family; second he must cut off his own self-will; and third, he must resist the vainglory that follows upon obedience. "Go out from their midst and be separate, and do not embrace the depravity of the world, says the Lord" (2 Cor 6:17). . . . Whenever, after our renunciation, demons induce in us memories of our parents and our brothers and sisters, causing warm affection to arise in our hearts, let us arm ourselves with prayer against them, and kindle within us the reminder of eternal fire, so that we may quench the untimely flicker of that memory from our hearts. If someone believes that he is impassible toward something, and yet distresses over losing possession of it, he is completely deceiving himself. As for those young men frantic for erotic bodily love and for the enjoyment of food while still wanting to pursue the monastic regimen, let them train themselves in all vigilance and prayer, and prevail over luxury, and desist from wickedness, lest their end become worse than their beginning. . . .

Step 3: On Exile

Exile is leaving behind, without looking back, everything in one's homeland that impedes him in pursuing the goal of true piety. Exile is a way of life deprived of freedom, an unknown wisdom, an unheralded understanding, a hidden life, an unobservable goal. Exile is unseen reflection, an appetite for lowliness, a desire for confinement, a longing for godly living, an abundance of passionate love, a repudiation of vainglory, a depth of silence. . . . If, as the Lord said, every prophet is without honor in his own country (John 4:44), then we should be careful lest our exile itself become the cause of vainglory. For exile is separation from everything for the sake of concentrating our thinking inseparably on God. Exile both loves and enacts insatiable compunction. An exile is a fugitive from all attachments to relatives and others. . . .

Detachment is good, and exile is its mother. Whoever goes into exile for the Lord's sake no longer has attachments, so that he will not appear deluded by his passions. Once you go into exile, you may no longer reach back for the world, otherwise your passions will be bound to recur.

3.

Christianity as a Rule of Life

INTRODUCTION

The texts in this and the preceding chapter bleed together insofar as they all relate to boundaries between Christians and "the world." Neither sequestering itself as an isolationist sect nor seeking mere legitimation under the canopy of Roman religious diversity proved a satisfactory option for Christianity. Ultimately the only viable alternative was for the churches to work toward maximal solidarity in doctrine and practice, and on that basis to confront Roman culture with as coherent a witness as possible to the uniqueness and appeal of their faith. Marking boundaries with the world was part of the struggle, then, but positively articulating what set Christians apart, not only in word but also in deed, was likewise decisive.

As I noted in the volume introduction, Christian behavior in the early churches required learning morality by imitation of exemplary figures. But that does not mean that explicit "rules" were of no avail. How could they not still be effectual when the Bible itself is full of straightforward commands and precepts? Indeed, Wayne Meeks highlights a whole "grammar" of behavioral obligation appropriated by the early Christians.[1] Beyond the New Testament, the anonymously authored *Didache* [3.1],

---

1. Meeks, *Origins of Christian Morality*, 66–90.

possibly as early as the late first century, begins precisely by confronting actual or prospective believers with a fork in their road. There is the way of life (Christ) and the way of death (the Devil), but no middle path. Commandments from the Decalogue (Exod 20:1–17) are combined with mandates from Jesus's Sermon on the Mount to delineate the non-negotiable terms of obedience and faithfulness to the Christian gospel. The author clearly has no fear of Christianity devolving into legalism; on the contrary, the commandments for the Christian life are means of grace, insofar as the Lord himself is present when the church's leaders issue them. Some of the *Didache*'s emphases echo in the *Apology* of the second-century writer Aristides of Athens [3.2], whose concern was to impress pagans with the profound discipline of Christians manifest in their clear-cut moral commitments.

The excerpts that I have included from Tertullian's disciplinary and ethical writings [3.3.1–3] show another stage in the attempt to advance Christianity as a rule of life. A lawyer by training, Tertullian proved to be an expert casuist, applying Scripture and traditional Christian moral teaching to individual cases of conscience arising in Christians' experience. Should a Christian engage in a trade or profession that even remotely or indirectly supported pagan idolatry [3.3.1]? Tertullian sought to prohibit this, appealing to the example of the Magi who, as professional astrologers, followed a star in order to honor the young Christ but then repudiated astrology by "returning another way" (Matt 2:12) to their homeland after their encounter with the Messiah. Could a Christian in good conscience attend the theatre or the games, which were such hotbeds of idolatry [3.3.2]? Tertullian's negative answer was fairly typical. Should a Christian woman not exercise extreme scruples in the ways that she adorned herself in public [3.3.3]? Or as Clement of Alexandria further asked, was it not incumbent on Christians (even if freed from Jewish dietary laws) to adhere to a modest diet in order to be an example of conquering gluttony and carnality [3.4]?

The sample text from Caesarius of Arles [3.5], much further down the road historically, gives us a glimpse of how Christian bishops in late antiquity continued to have to remind their congregations of their practical obligations and the basic rules of

Christian conduct. Inculcating the Creed and the Lord's Prayer, regularly going to church and paying full attention, consistently giving tithes, spurning residual scandalous practices from the pagan past—all of these were crucial for believers living in a society still very much transitioning in the embrace of Christianity. In the monastic tradition, too, specific rules of conduct were not to be abandoned; quite the contrary, they were to be compiled and made constitutional for monastic communities. Ultimately the most influential monastic *regula* from antiquity, the sixth-century *Rule of St. Benedict* of Nursia (Italy), set forth numerous moral precepts for monastic life [3.6], many of which commended themselves to non-monastic Christians as well.

THE TEXTS

3.1 *The Didache*[2]

1. There are two ways, one of life and one of death, and the two ways greatly differ. The way of life is as follows: First, you shall love the God who created you, and second, your neighbor as yourself; and whatever you do not want to be done to you, do not do that to another (cf. Matt 22:37–39; Deut 6:5; Lev 19:18). These words instruct the following: Bless those who curse you, and pray for your enemies, and fast for the sake of those who persecute you. For what grace is there in loving those who love you? Do not even the gentiles do the same? But for your part love those who hate you, and you will have no enemy (Luke 6:27–28, 32–33, 35). Desist from carnal and bodily desires (cf. 1 Pet 2:11). If anyone strikes you on your right cheek, turn to him the other cheek too (Matt 5:39) and you will be perfect (cf. Matt 5:48). If someone presses you to go with her one mile, go with her two (Matt 5:41). If anyone takes your coat, give him your shirt also. If anyone takes from you what is yours, do not refuse it to him (Luke 6:29). You cannot do so. Give to everyone who asks you, and do not decline (Luke 6:30), for the Father

---

2. Translated from the Greek text edited by Michael Holmes, *The Apostolic Fathers*, 3rd ed. (Grand Rapids: Baker Academic, 2007), 344–52.

desires that we give to all from the gifts he has bestowed. Blessed is the one who gives according to God's commandment, for that person is blameless. Woe to the one who receives; for if anyone receives out of need, he or she is innocent; but the one who receives apart from need will have to explain why he or she took the goods and to what purpose; and being confined, that person will be examined about his or her deeds, and will not be released until paying back every last cent (cf. Matt 5:26; Luke 12:59). But concerning this it was also said, "Let your alms sweat in your hands until you know to whom to give it" (cf. Sir 12:1–7).

2. The second commandment of the teaching is this: You shall not murder, or commit adultery (Exod 20:13-14), or indulge in pederasty, or commit fornication. You shall not steal (Exod 20:15). You shall not employ magic or delve into sorcery. You shall not perform an abortion or commit infanticide. You shall not covet your neighbor's possessions (Exod 20:17), or commit perjury, or bear false witness (Exod 20:16). You shall not slander or hold a grudge. You shall not be duplicitous or double-tongued, for to be double-tongued is a death trap. Your speech shall not be false or vain, but filled out with action. You shall not be greedy or given to extortion. You shall not be a hypocrite or malicious or haughty. You shall not plot evil devices against your neighbor. You shall hate no one, but reprove some, pray for others, and love still others more than your own soul.

3. My child, flee from every evil and anything that looks like evil. Do not become angry, for anger leads to murder. Do not be jealous or contentious or wrathful, for all these can generate murders. My child, do not be lustful, for lust leads to fornication. Do not be foul-mouthed or let your eyes wander, for these spawn adultery. My child, do not be an augur, since this leads to idolatry; do not be a charmer or astrologer or one who purifies by magical arts, and do not even wish to watch them, for idolatry derives from them all. My child, do not be a liar, since falsehood leads to stealing. Do not be greedy or conceited, for these too cause one to steal. My child, do not be a complainer, since it leads to blasphemy. Do not be self-willed or viciously minded, for blasphemies come from these as well. Instead be meek, for

the meek will inherit the earth (Matt 5:5). Be patient, merciful, guileless, tranquil, and good, reverencing always the words that you have heard. Do not exalt yourself or allow your soul to become rash. Your soul should not be hobnobbing with the elite but dwelling with the righteous and humble. Accept as good whatever befalls you, in the knowledge that nothing happens apart from God. . . .

4. Night and day, my child, remember the one who speaks God's word to you, and esteem him as if he were the Lord himself. For whenever his authority is communicated, the Lord is present. You shall furthermore seek out company of the saints so that you can rely on their words. You shall not foment division, and you shall pacify those who quarrel. You shall judge justly, and not play favorites when you reprove transgressions and not waver with your rulings. Be not one who reaches out the hands to receive but withdraws them when it comes to giving. If you acquire something by the work of your own hands, you shall give a ransom for your sins. You shall not hesitate to give or complain when you do give, for you will recognize who is the good paymaster of the reward. You shall not turn away from someone in need, but share all you have with your brother or sister, not considering it your own. For if you are a people who share in the imperishable, how much more you will share perishable things! You shall not hold back your hand from your son or daughter, but from the time they are young you shall teach them the fear of God. You shall not, in anger, issue commands to your male or female slave (they hope in the same God as you!), lest they stop fearing the God who rules over you both. For he comes to call us not on the basis of standing but those whom the Spirit has prepared. And you slaves shall be submissive to your masters with respect and fear, since the master symbolizes God. You shall despise all hypocrisy and anything unpleasing to the Lord. You shall not neglect the Lord's commandments but keep what you have received, neither adding to nor subtracting from them. In church you shall confess your sins and not enter into prayer with a bad conscience. This is the way of life.

5. The way of death, meanwhile, is as follows: first, it is evil and fully accursed, characterized by murders, adulteries, lusts, fornications, thefts, idolatries, magical crafts, sorceries, robberies, false testimonies, hypocrisies, duplicity, deceit, arrogance, malice, self-will, greed, a foul mouth, jealousy, overconfidence, haughtiness, and pretentiousness. Those who persecute good people follow the way of death, as do those who despise truth, love falsehood, fail to know the reward of righteousness, and fail to cling to the good and to righteous judgment. They are the ones vigilant not for good but for evil, being alien from gentleness and patience, loving vanities, pursuing payback, showing no mercy to the poor, or toiling for the oppressed. They are those who do not know the one who created them, who murder children, corrupt God's creation, turn away from the needy, oppress the afflicted, advocate for the wealthy, and are lawless judges of the poor, sinful through and through. May you be rescued, my children, from all these things!

3.2 Aristides of Athens, *Apology*[3]

15. Now the Christians, O king, by going about and seeking have found the truth, and as we have comprehended from their writings they are nearer to the truth and to exact knowledge than the rest of the peoples. For they know and believe in God, the Maker of heaven and earth, in whom are all things and from whom are all things (cf. Rom 11:36; 1 Cor 8:6; Col 1:16; Heb 1:2): he who has no other god as his fellow: from whom they have received those commandments which they have engraved on their minds, which they keep in the hope and expectation of the world to come. On this account they do not commit adultery or fornication, nor bear false witness (cf. Exod 20:14, 16), nor deny a deposit, nor covet what is not theirs (Exod 20:17). They honor father and mother (Exod 20:12); they do good to those who are their neighbors, and when they are judges they judge uprightly; and they do not worship idols in the form of

---

3. Translated from the Syriac version by J. Rendell Harris, *The Apology of Aristides*, Texts and Studies 1 (Cambridge: Cambridge University Press, 1891), 48–51. Modified and updated.

man (Exod 20:3–6; 1 Cor 8:4). Whatever they do not wish that others should do to them, they do not practice toward anyone (Matt 7:12), and they do not eat of the meats of idol sacrifices (1 Cor 8:1–13), for they are undefiled. And those who grieve, them they comfort, and make them their friends; and they do good to their enemies. And their wives, O king, are pure as virgins, and their daughters modest; and their men abstain from all unlawful wedlock and from all impurity, in the hope of the recompense that is to come in another world. But as for their servants or handmaids, or their children if any of them have any, they persuade them to become Christians for the love that they have towards them; and when they have become so, they call them without distinction brothers and sisters. They do not worship strange gods; and they walk in all humility and kindness, and falsehood is not found among them; and they love one another. They do not turn away their countenance from the widows; and they rescue the orphan from him who does the orphan violence. The one who has means gives to the one who has not, without grudging; and when Christians see the stranger they bring that person to their dwellings, and rejoice over that person as over a true brother or sister; for they do not call brothers or sisters those who are after the flesh, but those who are in the spirit and in God. But when one of their poor passes away from the world, and any of them sees him, then he provides for his burial according to his ability; and if they hear that any of their number is imprisoned or oppressed for the name of their Messiah, all of them provide for his or her needs, and if it is possible that the prisoner may be delivered, they deliver him or her.

And if there is among them a one that is poor or needy, and they have not an abundance of necessaries, Christians fast two or three days that they may supply the needy with their necessary food. And they observe scrupulously the commandments of their Messiah, living honestly and soberly, as the Lord their God commanded them. Every morning and at all hours on account of the goodness of God toward them they praise and laud him: and over their food and over their drink they render him thanks. And if any righteous person of their number passes away from the world they rejoice and give thanks to God, and they follow his or her body, as if it were moving from one place to another.

And when a child is born to any one of them, they praise God, and if again by chance it dies in its infancy, they praise God mightily, as for one who has passed through the world without sins. And if again they see that one of their number has died in his iniquity or in her sins, they weep bitterly and sigh, as over one who is about to go to punishment. Such is the ordinance of the law of the Christians, O king, and such their conduct.

16. As people who know God, Christians ask from him petitions which are proper for him to give and for them to receive; and thus they accomplish the course of their lives. And because they acknowledge the goodness of God towards them, behold, on account of them there flows forth the beauty that is in the world. And truly they are of the number of those that have found the truth by going about and seeking it, and as far as we have comprehended, we have understood that they only are near to the knowledge of the truth.

But the good deeds which they do, they do not proclaim in the ears of the multitude, and they take care that no one shall perceive them, and hide their gift, as one who has found a treasure and hides it. And they labor to become righteous as those that expect to see their Messiah and receive from him the promises made to them with great glory. . . . And I have no doubt that the world stands by reason of the intercession of Christians.

3.3 Tertullian: Excerpts from His Disciplinary and Ethical Works

3.3.1 *On Idolatry*[4]

9. Among the ways to make a living we also observe certain professions liable to idolatry. We should not even have to mention astrologers, but since a man has lately challenged us, defending his right to continue in that profession, I shall briefly address it.

---

4. Translated from the Latin text edited by J. H. Waszink and J. C. M. van Winden, *Tertullianus: De Idololatria*, Supplements to *Vigiliae Christianae* 1 (Leiden: Brill, 1987), 34–36, 44.

I am not alleging that this man worships the idols whose names he has inscribed in the heavens and to whom he has attributed all God's power. Nor am I suggesting that people, under the presumption that we are ruled by the immutable dominion of the stars, assume that seeking God is not a requirement. I am only proposing that it is those angels who deserted God, being lovers of women, who also introduced this [astrological] curiosity, and for this reason have been condemned by God. O the divine sentence which, unyielding, reaches even down to the earth, and to which even the ignorant bear witness! Astrologers are banned just like their angels. The city [of Rome] and all Italy are forbidden to the astrologers, just as heaven is off limits to their angels. The same penalty is imposed for disciples and teachers alike.

But, we hear, "Magi came from the East" (Matt 2:1). And we know the association between Magi and astrologers. Interpreters of the stars were thus the first ones to announce the birth of Christ, the first to give him gifts. I suppose that with this reputation, they bound Christ to them. What then? Will the piety of those Magi thereby cover for astrologers now? Shall we simply infer that astrology now has Christ as its subject, observing and preaching the star of Christ, not of Saturn and Mars and any other being from the same order of the dead? In point of fact that science was allowed to endure only until the Gospel arrived, so that after Christ's birth no one would any longer interpret another's birth according to the stars. For the Magi also presented the infant Lord with incense, myrrh, and gold as a fitting termination of the worldly offerings and glory which Christ was about to do away with.

So it was not to keep Herod from pursuing them that the Magi were warned in a dream—doubtless by God's will—that they should return to their own country by a way different from the one they had already taken (Matt 2:12). But the true meaning of this was that they should not continue in their former ways. Herod did not track them down, not even knowing that they had left by a different way, since he also did not know the way by which they had originally come. We are thus obliged to interpret "way" here as way of life and doctrine. It was in this sense that the Magi were commanded henceforth to proceed by another route. . . .

12. It is wrong for us to ease our consciences about the exigencies of human sustenance if, after sealing our [baptismal] faith, we say, "I have no way to make a living." I will now respond to this abrupt proposition more fully. It is expressed too late. This person should have pondered it ahead of time, taking the example of the exceedingly prudent builder (cf. Luke 14:28–29) who first calculates the cost along with the means at his disposal, lest once he begin the project he have to quit and be ashamed. But now too you have the Lord's own statements and examples removing from you any and all excuses. For what do you say? "I shall be needy!" But the Lord calls the poor happy (cf. Matt 5:3; Luke 6:20). "I will have no food!" "Do not think about food!" (Matt 6:25), and as for clothing we have the example of the lilies (Matt 6:28). "My work was my subsistence!" And yet everything you have should be sold with the proceeds distributed to the poor (Luke 18:22; cf. Matt 19:21). "But my children and posterity must be provided for!" "No one who puts his hand to the plow and looks back is fit" for work (Luke 9:62). "But I was under contract!" "No one can serve two masters!" (Matt 6:24). If you want to be the Lord's disciple, you must take up your cross and follow him (Luke 14:27; cf. Matt 10:38), that is, take up poverty and torment, or your body alone, which has the form of a cross. Parents, spouses, and children will have to be left behind for God's sake (Matt 19:29). Do you doubt this of the occupations, trades, and professions even on account of children and parents?

3.3.2 *On the Spectacles*[5]

15. Dealing with the matter of the places [theatres, etc.], we have already mentioned above that they do not contaminate us of themselves, but on account of what is done in them, that is, once

---

5. Translated by Rudolph Arbesmann, *Tertullian: Disciplinary, Moral and Ascetical Works*, Fathers of the Church, vol. 40 (Washington, DC: Catholic University of America Press, 1959), 83–86. Reprinted by permission of the Catholic University of America Press.

these places have imbibed contamination by such actions, they spit it out again to the same degree on others. So much, then, as we have said, for the main charge: idolatry.

Now let us also point out that the other characteristics of the things which are going on at the spectacles are all opposed to God. God has given us the command both to deal with the Holy Spirit in tranquility, gentleness, quiet, and peace, inasmuch as, in accordance with the goodness of his nature, he is tender and sensitive, and also not to vex him by frenzy, bitterness of feeling, anger, and grief (cf. Eph 4:30–31). How, then, can the Holy Spirit have anything to do with the spectacles? There is no spectacle without violent agitation of the soul. For, where you have pleasure, there is also desire which gives pleasure its savor. And where, in turn, you have rivalry, there also are frenzy and bitterness of feeling and anger and grief and other effects that spring from them, and, moreover, are incompatible with our moral discipline. For, even if a man enjoys spectacles modestly and soberly, as befits his rank, age, and natural disposition, he cannot go to them without his mind being roused and his soul being stirred by some unspoken agitation. No one ever approaches a pleasure such as this without passion; no one experiences this passion without its damaging effects. These very effects are incitements to passion. On the other hand, if the passion ceases, there is no pleasure, and he who goes where he gains nothing is convicted of foolishness. But I think that foolishness also is foreign to us. Is it, further, not true that a man really condemns himself when he has taken his place among those whose company he does not want and whom, at any rate, he confesses to detest? It is not enough to refrain from such acts, unless we also shun those who commit them. "If thou didst see a thief," says holy Scripture, "thou didst run with him" (Ps 49:18). Would that we did not live in the world with them! Still, we are separated from them in the things of the world. For the world is God's, but the things of the world are the Devil's.

16. Since, then, frenzy is forbidden us, we are debarred from every type of spectacle, including the circus, where frenzy rules supreme. Look at the populace, frenzied even as it comes to the show, already in violent commotion, blind, wildly excited over

its wagers. The praetor is too slow for them; all the time their eyes are rolling as though in rhythm with the lots he shakes up in his urn. Then they await the signal with bated breath; one outcry voices the common madness. Recognize the madness from their foolish behavior. "He has thrown it!" they shout; everyone tells everybody else what all of them have seen just that moment. This I take as proof of their blindness: they do not see what has been thrown—a signal cloth, they think—but it is the symbol of the Devil hurled headlong from on high. Accordingly, from such beginnings the affair progresses to outbursts of fury and passion and discord and to everything forbidden to the priests of peace. Next come curses, insults without any justified reason for the hatred, and rounds of applause without the reward of affection. What are the partakers in all this—no longer their own masters—likely to achieve for themselves? At best, the loss of their self-control. They are saddened by another's bad luck; they rejoice in another's success. What they hope for and what they dread has nothing to do with themselves, and so their affection is to no purpose and their hatred is unjust. Or are we, perhaps, permitted to love without cause any more than to hate without cause? God who bids us to love our enemies certainly forbids us to hate even with cause; God who commands us to bless those who curse us does not permit us to curse even with cause (cf. Matt 5:44; Rom 12:14). But what is more merciless than the circus, where they do not even spare their rulers or their fellow citizens? If any of these frenzies of the circus become the faithful elsewhere, then it will be lawful also in the circus; but, if nowhere, then neither in the circus.

3.3.3 *On Women's Adornment*, Book 2[6]

5. These suggestions are not made to you, of course, to be developed into an entire crudity and wildness of appearance; nor are we seeking to persuade you of the good of squalor and slovenliness; but of the limit and norm and just measure of cultivation of the person. There must be no overstepping of that line to

---

6. Translated by Sydney Thelwall, *Tertullian, Part Fourth*, Ante-Nicene Fathers, vol. 4 (Edinburgh: T&T Clark, 1885), 20–21. Revised and updated.

which simple and sufficient refinements limit their desires—that line which is pleasing to God. For they who rub their skin with medicaments, stain their cheeks with rouge, make their eyes prominent with antimony, sin against him. To them, I suppose, the plastic skill of God is displeasing! In their own persons, I suppose, they convict, they censure, the Artificer of all things! For they censure him when they amend, when they add to [God's work], taking these their additions, of course, from the adversary artificer. That adversary artificer is the Devil. For who would show the way to change the *body*, but he who by wickedness transfigured a human being's *spirit*? He it is, undoubtedly, who adapted ingenious devices of this kind; that in your persons it may be apparent that you, in a certain sense, do violence to God. Whatever is *born* is the work of God. Whatever, then, is *plastered on* is the Devil's work. To superinduce on a divine work Satan's ingenuities, how criminal is it! Our servants borrow nothing from our personal enemies: soldiers eagerly desire nothing from the foes of their own general; for, to demand for (your own) use anything from the adversary of him in whose hand you exist, is a transgression. Shall a Christian be assisted in anything by that Evil One? If so, I know not whether this name (of "Christian") will continue (to belong) to him; for he will be *his* in whose teaching he eagerly desires to be instructed. But how alien from your schoolings and professions are (these things)! How unworthy the Christian name, to wear a fictitious face, (you,) on whom simplicity in every form is enjoined!—to lie in your appearance, (you,) to whom (lying) with the tongue is not lawful!—to seek after what is another's, (you,) to whom is delivered (the precept of) abstinence from what is another's!—to commit adultery in your very appearance, you who make modesty your study! Think, blessed sisters, how will you keep God's precepts if you shall not keep in your own persons his lineaments? . . .

8. Of course, now, I, a man, as being envious of women, am banishing them quite from their own (domains). Are there, in our case too, some things which, in respect of the sobriety we are to maintain on account of the fear due to God, are disallowed? If it is true (as it is) that in men, for the sake of women

(just as in women for the sake of men), there is implanted, by a defect of nature, the will to please; and if this sex of ours acknowledges to itself deceptive trickeries of form peculiarly its own—(such as) to cut the beard too sharply; to pluck it out here and there; to shave round about (the mouth); to arrange the hair, and disguise its agedness by dyes; to remove all the incipient down all over the body; to fix (each particular hair) in its place with (some) womanly pigment; to smooth all the rest of the body by the aid of some rough powder or other: then, further, to take every opportunity for consulting the mirror; to gaze anxiously into it—while yet, when (once) the knowledge of God has put an end to all wish to please by means of voluptuous attraction, all these things are rejected as frivolous, as hostile to modesty. For where God is, there modesty is; there is sobriety her assistant and ally. How, then, shall we practice modesty without its instrumental mean, that is, without sobriety? How, moreover, shall we bring sobriety to bear on the discharge of (the functions of) modesty, unless seriousness in appearance and in countenance, and in the general aspect of the entire man, mark our carriage?

3.4 Clement of Alexandria, *The Instructor*, Book 2[7]

1. Whenever reason[8] leads one away from externals and from bodily concerns to the concerns of intellect, and thus schools that person in the contemplation of humanity's natural attributes, he or she will know not to be preoccupied with externals, and to cleanse the eye of the soul and to sanctify the flesh itself. For being purged clean of those things whereby a human being is still dust, what else would she or he have more conducive to proceeding on the way to the apprehension of God?

There are other people who live to eat, indeed just like irrational animals. For them, life is nothing other than their belly. The Instructor [Christ the Logos], on the other hand, advises us

---

7. Translated from the Greek text edited by Miroslav Marcovich, *Clementi Alexandrini Paedagogus* (Leiden: Brill, 2002), 65–68.

8. When Clement uses the Greek *logos* in this work, it may refer to reason itself and/or the indwelling divine Logos (Word) who is the Instructor of the soul through reason.

to eat in order to live. Eating food is not our primary activity, and pleasure not our objective. Food is merely for our earthly livelihood, which the Logos is educating toward incorruption. So our food should be screened. It should be plain, simple, and, in keeping with truth, suitable for simple and unprovocative children. It should be useful for survival, not for self-indulgence; and that survival consists in two things only, health and strength, and to these a plain diet is most conducive, useful for digestion and restricting weight-gain. From these come growth, health, and proper strength, not the abnormal, dangerous, wretched kind of strength that athletes acquire by their compulsory feeding. Therefore too many varieties of foods are to be rejected, as these can do all sorts of damage, such as bad bodily habits, stomach disorders, perversion of one's sense of taste by some ill-fated cooking venture and useless attempt at making pastries. Some have the nerve to call such indulgence in luxuries "food," even when it devolves into harmful pleasures. The Delian physician Antiphanes declared that one of the causes of disease was indulgence in a variety of foods. All the while there are those who, in their multifaceted vanity, do not like the truth, renouncing a sound diet and obsessing over delicacies from overseas.

As for me, I feel pity for them in their disease, as they shamelessly sing the praises of their delicacies, going to every length to acquire lampreys from the Straits of Sicily, eels from Maeander, goat-kids from Melos, mullets from Sciathos, mussels from Pelorus, oysters from Abydos. . . .

Gluttony knows no limit with human beings. It runs them aground on pastries, honey-cakes, and sweetmeats, invents a plethora of desserts, and hunts for all sorts of dishes. In my view such a person is all mouth and nothing else. Scripture says, "Do not desire the delicacies of the rich, for these pertain to a false and shameful life" (Prov 23:3). Gluttons are attached to their delicacies, which a little later the privy receives, while for us it is necessary to seek after heavenly food and to subjugate the belly under heaven, and all the more so the things dear to the belly, which, as the Apostle says, "God will destroy" (1 Cor 6:13), rightly cursing gluttonous desires. "Food is for the belly" (1 Cor 6:13), and on it depends this carnal and destructive life of ours.
. . .

3.5 Caesarius of Arles, *Sermon* 13[9]

1. I entreat you, beloved brothers and sisters, to be more attentive to why we are Christians and bear the cross of Christ on our foreheads. For we must know that it is not sufficient for us to have accepted the name "Christian" if we do not perform Christian deeds. . . .

2. And in order for you to be able, with God's help, to achieve this, maintain peace on your own and recall to harmony those who sow discord. Flee from falsehood. Be in dread of perjury as perpetual death. Do not be willing to bear false witness or to commit theft (cf. Exod 20:15–16). Above all else, as I mentioned earlier, give alms to the poor as your means will allow. Bring offerings to be consecrated on the altar. Anyone who has the means to do so should blush to piggyback on someone else's offering. Those who can should donate either candles or oil that can be used in lamps. Know the Creed and the Lord's Prayer by heart, and teach them to your children; for I do not know how one can outwardly call himself a Christian if he neglects mastering the few lines of Creed or the Lord's Prayer.

Be aware that you appeared in God's presence as guarantors for the children you received in baptism; so always you are to chasten and correct them so that they will live in chastity, justice, and sobriety. . . .

3. Go to church every Lord's Day. For if the hapless Jews are so devout in celebrating their Sabbath that they engage in no mundane labor on that day, how much more should Christians dedicate themselves to God alone on the Lord's Day and gather in church for the salvation of their souls! And when you assemble for church, pray for your sins. Do not foment strife or incite quarrels and scandals, for whoever does so when coming to church only injures herself in the contention where she might heal herself with prayer. When you stand in church, do not engage in chatter but listen patiently to the divine readings

---

9. Translated from the Latin text edited by Germain Morin, reproduced in Marie-José Delage, ed., *Césaire d'Arles: Sermons au peuple*, Sources Chrétiennes, no. 175 (Paris: Cerf, 1971), 416, 418–20, 420–22.

from Scripture, for whoever wants to engage in idle chatter in church will have to give account of the evil done to himself and others, not listening to the word of God himself nor allowing others to do. Pay tithes to the church from your meager earnings.

Whoever is proud should be humble. Whoever committed adultery should be chaste. Whoever was in the habit of stealing from others or invading their property should begin giving to the poor from his own means. Whoever is envious should be benevolent, and the ill-tempered, patient. Whoever has done harm to another should promptly seek forgiveness; but if he himself is done harm, he should promptly pardon it. . . .

5. Although I believe that, by divine inspiration, and thanks to your own remonstrances, the useless custom left over from profane pagan religious observances has been removed from these precincts, nevertheless if you know people who still engage in that most sordid and shameful act of dressing up like hags or fawns, chastise them so harshly that they will repent of having committed this sacrilege. If, when there is a lunar eclipse, you know of any people who still shriek, then rebuke them by denouncing the gravity of the sin they commit when they are confident that by their clamoring and maleficent sacrilege they can protect the moon itself, which is obscured at certain times by God's own command. Further, if you see people who still make solemn vows to springs or to trees, and, as I said earlier, consult magicians, diviners, or charmers, bedecking themselves or their family with sinister phylacteries, magical insignias, herbs, or amber charms, reproach them severely, since whoever commits this evil loses the sacramental grace of baptism. Because we have heard that the Devil himself so dupes some people that the men do no work and the women no weaving on Thursdays, let us declare before God and his angels that whoever wants to do this shall be damned to the place where the Devil will burn him, unless he emends this grave sacrilege by prolonged and rigorous penance. I have no doubt that these wretched and miserable people, who cease working on Thursdays in honor of Jupiter, are neither ashamed nor fearful of working on the Lord's Day. So vigorously rebuke those whom you know that still do this;

and if they refuse to change their ways, do not allow them to have conversation with you or to be your table guests. . . .

3.6 *Rule of St. Benedict* 4 ("The Instruments of Good Works")[10]

1. In the first place, to love the Lord God with the whole heart, the whole soul, the whole strength. 2. Then, one's neighbor as oneself. 3. Then not to murder. 4. Not to commit adultery. 5. Not to steal. 6. Not to covet. 7. Not to bear false witness. 8. To honor all. 9. And not to do to another what one would not have done to oneself. 10. To deny oneself in order to follow Christ. 11. To chastise the body. 12. Not to become attached to pleasures. 13. To love fasting. 14. To relieve the poor. 15. To clothe the naked. 16. To visit the sick. 17. To bury the dead. 18. To help in trouble. 19. To console the sorrowing. 20. To become a stranger to the world's ways. 21. To prefer nothing to the love of Christ. 22. Not to give way to anger. 23. Not to nurse a grudge. 24. Not to entertain deceit in one's heart. 25. Not to give a false peace. 26. Not to forsake charity. 27. Not to swear, for fear of perjuring oneself. 28. To utter truth from heart and mouth. 29. Not to return evil for evil. 30. To do no wrong to anyone, and to bear patiently wrongs done to oneself. 31. To love one's enemies. 32. Not to curse those who curse us, but rather to bless them. 33. To bear persecution for justice's sake. 34. Not to be proud. 35. Not addicted to wine. 36. Not a great eater. 37. Not drowsy. 38. Not lazy. 39. Not a grumbler. 40. Not a detractor. 41. To put one's hope in God. 42. To attribute to God, and not to self, whatever good one sees in oneself. 43. But to recognize always that the evil is one's own doing, and to impute it to oneself. 44. To fear the Day of Judgment. 45. To be in dread of hell. 46. To desire eternal life with all the passion of the spirit. 47. To keep death daily before one's eyes. 48. To keep constant guard over the actions of one's life. 49. To know for certain that God sees one everywhere. 50. When evil thoughts come into one's heart, to dash them against Christ immediately. 51. And to man-

---

10. Translated by Leonard Doyle (Collegeville, MN: Order of St. Benedict, 1938), 14–15.

ifest them to one's spiritual guardian. 52. To guard one's tongue against evil and depraved speech. 53. Not to love much talking. 54. Not to speak useless words or words that move to laughter. 55. Not to love much or boisterous laughter. 56. To listen willingly to holy reading. 57. To devote oneself frequently to prayer. 58. Daily in one's prayers, with tears and sighs, to confess one's past sins to God, and to amend them for the future. 59. Not to fulfill the desires of the flesh; to hate one's own will. 60. To obey in all things the commands of the Abbot or Abbess even though they (which God forbid) should act otherwise, mindful of the Lord's precept, "Do what they say, but not what they do." 61. Not to wish to be called holy before one is holy; but first to be holy, that one may be truly so called.

4.

Divine Paideia and the Quest for Moral Wisdom

INTRODUCTION

The idea that God uses many means to instruct his people morally and religiously is deeply biblical. The Hebrew Scriptures reiterate that God chastens, admonishes, and educates his people not only directly through Torah, or through the timely word of the Prophets, but also through the banes and blessings of sheer experience, as we find in Wisdom texts like Job, Ecclesiastes, and Wisdom of Solomon. For the writer of the Epistle to the Hebrews, which is largely a sermon on Christian endurance in the light of Christ's own supreme sacrifice, God's discipline (*paideia*) amid hardship is both severe and redemptive (cf. Heb 12:3–13). Famously for Paul, God's wisdom revealed itself precisely in the foolishness of the cross, which put worldly wisdom to shame (1 Cor 1:18–2:9), such that the only wise course for Christians is a cruciform life, finding power in weakness and in self-sacrificial love. For Paul, Christ is not simply the exemplar of this wisdom; he *is* in himself the very Wisdom of God (1 Cor 1:24, 30), and the Spirit must intervene to initiate believers in the depths of this wisdom, instilling in them the "mind of Christ" (1 Cor 2:10–16).

Early Christian thinkers continued, in turn, to see God's *paideia* as exhibited in multiple forms and leading faithful souls toward multiple kinds of understanding. The texts in this chapter sample different aspects of the quest to apprehend divine wisdom for the moral and religious life. Clement of Alexandria (ca. 160–215), in a formal *logos protrepkikos* ("rhetorical exhortation"), appealed to "Greeks and barbarians" alike, all created in God's image, to join in the quest for perfect assimilation to God by embracing the ultimate wisdom of the Christian gospel [4.1.1]. He depicted the divine Logos as a transcendent and immanent (and intimate) instructor in godliness, wisdom, and salvation itself, and outlined the diverse methods of his pedagogy evidenced through the scriptural Word [4.1.2]. For Clement, the Logos instills divine *philosophia* in his disciples, and Clement's academic successor Origen (ca. 185–ca. 253) looked to make this superior wisdom the core curriculum of his own teaching in Alexandria and later in Caesarea Palestinae. In a letter to his student Gregory Thaumaturgus (ca. 210–260), Origen confirms the value of employing Greek arts and sciences as well as philosophy in interpreting scriptural revelation, using the biblical figure of "spoiling the Egyptians" [4.2]. Origen's approach is confirmed by Gregory in a panegyric on his teacher, detailing how Origen combined severity and gentleness in training up his students in philosophical and moral wisdom [4.3]. Clearly this teaching model was intended to mirror the Logos's own pedagogy—the Logos who is himself source of all truth, whether revealed through Scripture or through created nature.

The Cappadocian Fathers were great admirers of Clement and Origen, and carried forward their emphasis on the divine *paideia* operative through intense study of Scripture in the context of an appropriately humanistic education. Writing after Constantine, when the church was challenged to reassess its Greco-Roman cultural inheritance, Basil of Caesarea reiterated the legitimacy of selectively using pagan literary and philosophical sources that anticipated Christian truths [4.4]. Basil's younger brother Gregory of Nyssa credited their sister Macrina as an astute mentor in the ascetical *philosophia* central to his own moral and spiritual teaching. In the *Life of Macrina* [4.5.1], he recounted her crucial role in the household in converting their mother to the "philosophical" life and cultivating an ascetical community with their former maidservants. The brief excerpt from Gregory's *Dialogue on the Soul and Resurrection* [4.5.2] is merely the front end of an extended discussion between him and Macrina on anthropological and ascetical themes, including in this case the enormous problem of calibrating and modulating human emotions in the context of *philosophia*.

Not all divine wisdom, however, was conveyed in instructional or ascetical settings, as Gregory of Nazianzus (ca. 329–390) demonstrated in a speech occasioned by the "plague" of hail that had devastated lands in his father's diocese. God's discipline can be severe, as when he uses natural disasters and tragic events to teach Christians hard moral lessons, particularly in this case landowners who have oppressed the poor or pushed them off their land [4.6].

The last two selections are of a more reflective and meditative nature. Ephrem the Syrian (ca. 306–373), one of the most prolific theologians and poets of the Syriac Christian tradition, ponders in the third of his *Hymns on Paradise* [4.7] how the path to wisdom was already symbolically set out in Eden, where the tree of the knowledge of good and evil was strategically placed in the middle not simply as a prohibition but as a hedge or veil protecting the inner sanctuary of the garden. Abusing their freedom, Adam and Eve partook of the tree prematurely, and their newfound knowledge proved a vexation—implying that such knowledge is available only to those who are morally and spiritually prepared for it, the wisdom that is the "glory of the inner Tabernacle." Augustine at last provides a strong reminder from his rich treatise *On the Trinity* [4.8] that all the fullness of heavenly wisdom and earthly knowledge are present in Jesus Christ alone. Christ himself is the true object of the quest for wisdom.

THE TEXTS

4.1 Clement of Alexandria

4.1.1 *Exhortation to the Greeks*[1]

12. You come too, old man! Leave Thebes! Cast away your prophetic and Bacchic ecstasy and be led to the truth. I give you the wood [of Christ's cross] to lean on. Hurry Teiresias,[2] and have faith! You will have sight! Christ, through whom the eyes of the blind see again, shines on you more brightly than the sun. Night will flee from you; fire will fear you; and death will depart from you. Even if you cannot see Thebes, old-timer, you shall see heaven!

O truly holy mysteries! O light unfading! Torch in hand, I contemplate the heavens and God himself, and I am initiated as holy. The Lord gives instruction in the mysteries, and while illuminating initiates, seals them, entrusts them to the Father once they have believed, and guards them for eternity. Such are the revelries of my mysteries. If you wish, be a learner yourself, and you shall dance with the angels around the unbegotten, imperishable, and only true God, with the Word of God joining us in our hymn of praise. Jesus the eternal, the one great High Priest of the only God, his Father, prays for and encourages humanity. "Hearken, you myriad peoples,[3] or rather, you the more reasonable of human beings, barbarians and Greeks alike. I beseech you, the whole human race, being your Creator by the Father's will. Come to me, so that you may be given status under the one God and the one Word of God; and do not excel the unreasoning beasts in reason alone, for among all mortal beings I grant

---

1. Translated from the Greek text edited by Miroslav Marcovich, *Clementis Alexandrini Protrepticus* (Leiden: Brill, 2015), 172–77.

2. This "old man," Teiresias, was the blind prophet who appeared in the Greek tragedies of Euripides, Sophocles, and Aeschylus, perhaps most famously as the bearer of divine judgment against the king in Sophocles's *Oedipus Rex*. Clearly for Clement, Teiresias epitomized the more redeemable characters in the works of the Greek poets, those who exposed pagan religious and moral bankruptcy.

3. Actually the words of Hector in Homer's *Iliad* 17.1.220, placed by Clement on Jesus's lips.

you alone the enjoyment of immortality. For I desire so much to grant you this grace, providing you with its perfect benefit of immortality. I grace you with reason, the knowledge of God, my very self to the fullest. For this I am; this God wills; this is unison; this is the Father's harmony, this is the Son, this is Christ; this is the Word of God, from the arms of the Lord; this is the power of the universe, the Father's will. Oh you who were all images [of God] but not all yet his likeness (cf. Gen 1:26), I want to restore you to the archetype, so that you too may become like me.[4] I will anoint you with oil through faith, by which you shed corruption, and display to you the bare form of righteousness, through which you ascend to God. Come unto me, all you who labor and are heavy-laden, and I will give you rest. Take my yoke upon you and learn from me, for I am gentle and humble in heart, and you shall find rest for your souls. For my yoke is easy and my burden is light (Matt 11:28–30)."

Let us hasten, let us run, we who are God's beloved, Godlike images of the Word. Let us hasten; let us run; let us take on his yoke; let us devote ourselves to incorruptibility; let us love Christ, the charioteer of humanity. Under the yoke he guided the colt and its parent (cf. Matt 21:1–7), and having yoked the team of humankind, he guides his chariot straight for immortality. He hastens toward God to fulfill clearly what he once spoke of only enigmatically. For having originally paraded into Jerusalem (cf. Matt 21:8–11), he has now penetrated the heavens (cf. Heb 9:24), a most spectacular sight for the Father: the eternal Son bringing victory. So let us men and women be ambitious for the good, and become friends of God; and let us lay hold of the greatest of goods: God and life. The Word is our helper. Let us have confidence in him and never again allow the longing for such things as silver, gold, and glory weigh upon us as much as the longing for the very Word of truth. For it is not at all pleasing to God himself if we make the least of what is of the greatest value and embrace the obvious outrages and ultimate impiety of ignorance, stupidity, sloth, and idolatry.

---

4. Like other Greek patristic authors, including Origen after him, Clement distinguished between the "image" (*eikōn*) of God naturally endowed in all human beings and the "likeness" (*homoiōsis*; lit. "assimilation") gained only through progress in virtuous living. Salvation and deification consist in perfecting this assimilation.

Not improperly do the children of the philosophers deem that the ignorant, in all their deeds, act profanely and impiously; furthermore they depict ignorance itself as a form of madness, and they confess that most human beings are nothing but mad. But now reason does not allow any room for doubting which is better, sanity or madness. Holding to the truth with all our strength we must use prudence to follow God and to consider all things his, which they indeed are. Having learned that we are the most excellent of his possessions, we should commit ourselves to God, loving the Lord and considering this our work for all our lives. If in fact "friends have all things in common,"[5] and the human being is a friend of God—beloved of God through the mediation of the Word, then all things become humanity's own, because all things are God's, and are common to both friends, God and humanity. So it is time for us to announce openly that only the God-fearer, the Christian, is rich, prudent, and noble, bearing the image of God along with the [acquired] likeness to God; and to state and believe that when one becomes "righteous and holy with prudence"[6] through Jesus Christ, he or she has already to that extent become like God. The prophet revealed that grace when he said, "I declare that you are all gods and sons of the Most High" (Ps 82:6). For he has adopted us—indeed us, not the recalcitrant—as the only ones by whom he wishes to be called Father. This is the status we enjoy as Christ's attendants:[7] as are the counsels, so are the words; as are the words, so are the acts; as are the deeds, so is the life—the auspicious life of all human beings who have come to acknowledge Christ....

4.1.2 *The Instructor*, Book 1[8]

9. So then with all his power, our divine Logos, Instructor of humanity, has devoted himself to saving his children, deploying every device of his wisdom: admonishing, censuring, chastising,

---

5. Plato, *Phaedrus* 279C; cf. Acts 2:44.

6. Plato, *Theaetetus* 176B.

7. A probable reminiscence of the subjects of divine Eros as Zeus's "attendants" in Plato, *Phaedrus* 252C.

8. Translated from the Greek text edited by Marcovich, *Clementis Alexandrini Paedagogus*, 46–57, 59, with emphasis added.

reproving, reproaching, threatening, healing, promising, showing favor, and, "as if binding with many reins,"[9] curbing our irrational human impulses. To put it briefly, the Lord deals with us just as we deal with our own children. As a book of Wisdom recommends, "Do you have children? Discipline them! Turn them from their youthful foolishness. Do you have daughters? Pay attention to their bodies, and do not brighten your face toward them" (Sir 7:23–24). And indeed, we do love our children, sons and daughters, exceedingly, and more than anything else. But whereas those who interact with another simply out of kindness actually do not love that person very much since they cause the person no stress, those who reprove another for his or her benefit, even if they cause pain in the short run, thereupon do that person everlasting good. The Lord projects not momentary pleasure, but future delight. So let us review the method of his philanthropic pedagogy using prophetic witnesses.

Admonition (nouthetēsis), then, is censure by provident care, intended to promote understanding. The Instructor employs admonition when, in the Gospel, he says, "How often did I wish to gather your children, just as a hen gathers her chicks under her wings, and you did not want it" (Matt 23:37).... Great is the proof of God's love for humanity, for while he clearly sees the shamefulness of his fugitive and rebellious people, he also calls them to repentance, announcing through Ezekiel the prophet, "Son of man, you dwell in the midst of scorpions; nevertheless, speak to them, in the event that they might hear" (Ezek 2:6–7). But to Moses he says, "Go and tell Pharaoh to let my people go, but I know that he will not let them go" (Exod 3:18–19). He manifests two things here: both his divinity in having foreknowledge, and his love of humanity in granting souls the occasion to repent of their own free will.... Thus while his solicitude exposes sin, he concomitantly points the way to salvation.

Censure (epitimēsis) is blame placed on shameful acts which then acclimates one to good deeds. The Instructor exhibits this method through Jeremiah: "'They became like lusty stallions, each one neighing for his neighbor's wife. Shall I not scrutinize

---

9. Quoted from Plato, *Laws* 7, 808D.

them?' says the Lord. 'Or shall my soul not seek vengeance on such a people as this?'" (Jer 5:8–9). The Instructor weaves everything with fear, because "the fear of the Lord is the beginning of understanding" (cf. Prov 1:7). . . .

Chastisement (*mempsis*) is rebuke heaped on the neglectful and careless. The Instructor deploys this pedagogical method through Isaiah, who says, "Hear, O heavens, and give ear, O earth, for the Lord has spoken. 'I have begotten children and exalted them, but they have rejected me. The ox knows his owner and the ass knows his master's crib, but Israel has not recognized me'" (Isa 1:2). . . .

Reproof (*epiplēxis*) is corrective admonition or penetrating rebuke, and the Instructor applies this therapy through Isaiah: "'Woe unto you, apostate children,' says the Lord, 'that you have made plans, but not through me, and agreements, but not through my Spirit'" (Isa 30:1). . . .

Reproach (*elenchos*) is publicly exposing sin and setting it in the sinner's midst. The Instructor uses this optimally as the requisite teaching method for those whose faith is waffling. As he says through Isaiah, "You have forsaken the Lord, and provoked the Holy One of Israel" (Isa 1:4), and through Jeremiah, "Heaven was appalled at this, and the earth shuddered more and more, for this people of mine have committed two evils: they forsook me, the fountain of living water; and they dug out for themselves cisterns that are cracked and will not be able to hold water" (Jer 2:12–13). . . . But softening the austerity and harshness of reproach, the Instructor says, through Solomon—and only tacitly hinting at the love for his children that marks his teaching—"My son, do not neglect the Lord's discipline, nor break down when you are reproached by him. For the Lord loves the one whom he disciplines, and punishes every son that he accepts" (Prov 3:11–12). . . .

Bringing one to his or her senses (*phrenōsis*) is rebuke that works to make one think. Neither does the Instructor hold back from this teaching method. As he says through Jeremiah, "How long shall I cry out, and they will not listen? Behold, their ears are uncircumcised" (Jer 6:10). O what blessed forbearance. . . .

Visitation (*episkopē*) is exceedingly harsh rebuke. The Instructor employs it this way in the Gospel: "Jerusalem, Jerusalem, you who kill the prophets and stone those who are sent to you... Your house is left to you desolate. I tell you, you shall not see me henceforth until you say: Blessed is he who comes in the name of the Lord" (Matt 23:37–39). If you do not accept his lovingkindness, you shall discover his authority.

Invective (*loidoria*) is intensified verbal rebuke, and the Instructor uses it as part of his medicine when he says through Isaiah, "Woe to you sinful nation, lawless sons, a people teeming with sins, wicked seed" (Isa 1:4). Again in the Gospel, he says through John, "Snakes! a viper's brood!" (cf. Matt 23:33).

Accusation (*engklēsis*) is the rebuke of wrongdoers. This is the teaching method deployed through David when he says, "A people whom I did not know served me, and at the hearing of the ear obeyed me, and foreign children lied to me and limped from their paths" (Ps 18:44–45). . . .

Bewailing one's fate (*mempsimoiria*) is latent rebuke, by artful aid administering salvation but in a veiled manner. The Instructor implemented this in the words of Jeremiah: "How did the city that was teeming with people remain solitary? It has become like a widow. A ruler among countries, it has turned into tribute. Weeping, she wept in the night" (Lam 1:1–2).

Ridicule (*diasursis*) is rebuke by disparagement. This too the Instructor employs to help us, as when he says through Jeremiah, "You took on the look of a harlot, and acted shamelessly toward all. And you did not, as it were, call me home, the one who is your Father and who originates your virginity?" (Jer 3:3–4). . . . By tactically insulting the virgin with the label of harlot, he in turn respectfully calls her back to holiness.

Righteous indignation (*katanemesēsis*) is lawful censure, or censure of ways of living that press beyond propriety. He educates us in this manner through Moses, when he asks, "Blameworthy children, crooked and perverted generation, is this how you requite the Lord? This is a foolish, not a wise people. Is this not the very Father who acquired you?" (Deut 32:5–6).

10. If, then, we have demonstrated how the Instructor's plan for reproving humanity is good and salutary, a necessary undertak-

ing of the Logos and suitable for bringing about repentance and the prevention of sin, we would next focus on the gentleness of the Logos. . . .

The Instructor makes use of *exhortation* (*protropē*) to what is [morally] useful when, through Solomon, he says, "You, O people, I exhort, and I lift my voice to the sons of men. Listen to me, for I am holy," and so on (Prov 8:4, 6).[10] He advises what is salutary, since *advice* (*symboulē*) is conducive to choosing or fleeing a course of action, as when the Instructor says through David, "Blessed is the one who has not walked by the counsel of the impious, nor stood in the way of sinners, nor sat on the seat of pestilences. His will abides rather in the law of the Lord" (Ps 1:1). Advice has three modes. The first is taking examples from times gone by, such as what the Hebrews suffered when they worshipped the idol of the golden calf (Exod 32:1–35), and what they suffered when they committed fornication or similar acts. The second mode of such advice provides reflections from present circumstances and is empirically grasped. As was said to those who asked the Lord, "Are you the Christ, or shall we look for another?" "Go and tell John that the blind see, the deaf hear, the lepers are cleansed, the dead are raised, and blessed is the one who has not been offended at me" (Matt 11:3–6). This was what David prophesied when he said, "Just as we heard, so also have we seen" (Ps 48:8). The third mode of advice draws from future events, bidding us to be on our guard for things about to happen, such as in the saying that those who fall into sin "shall be cast into outer darkness, and there they will weep and gnash their teeth" (Matt 8:12). And there are other passages of similar effect. So it is clear from this that the Lord accommodates any and every therapy to call humanity to salvation.

As well, with *consolation* (*paramythia*) he assuages sin, reducing lust while at once giving hope for salvation. For the Instructor says through Ezekiel's phrase, "If you return with all your heart and say, 'Father,' I will hear you as a holy people . . ." (cf. Ezek

10. In the preceding text [4.1.1] from the *Protrepticus*, the "appeal" to pagans to convert to true Wisdom is the divine Logos's own appeal, mediated through Clement's rhetoric and through exhortations drawn from Scripture; here we see Clement emphasizing that this same appeal (*protropē*) is a formal technique of the Logos's pedagogy as communicated through scriptural prophets and apostles.

18:21–23; 33:11; Deut 30:1–5). And elsewhere he says, "Come to me, all you who are weary and heavy-laden, and I will give you rest" (Matt 11:28), and the subsequent words that the Lord himself spoke. And as plain as day he calls people to goodness through Solomon, saying, "Blessed is the man who has found wisdom, and the mortal who has found prudence" (Prov 3:13).
. . .

There is yet another form of the Instructor's pedagogy, *blessing* (*makarismos*), as when he says through David, "Blessed is the one who does not sin, who will be like the tree planted close to the running waters, which will yield its fruit in due season and not lose its foliage (which also hints at the resurrection), and in everything that he does he will prosper" (Ps 1:1, 3). Such is what he wants us to be, so that we will be blessed. Then, by a comparison demonstrating the scales of justice, he adds, "But not so for the impious, not so! They are rather like the dust that the wind casts from off the surface of the ground" (Ps 1:4). . . .

The Instructor also calls us to knowledge (*gnōsis*),[11] saying through Jeremiah, "Had you walked in the way of God, you would dwell in peace forever" (Bar 3:13). Showing there the reward of knowledge, he entreats the prudent to passionate love of that knowledge and offers forgiveness to those who have gone astray. "Turn, turn, as a grape-gatherer to his basket" (Jer 6:9). Do you see the goodness of his justice in advising repentance? Through Jeremiah, moreover, he illumines truth for the errant: "Thus says the Lord, 'Stand at the roads and see, and ask for the Lord's everlasting paths. See what the good way is, and walk in it, and you shall find purification for your souls'" (Jer 6:16). . . .

11. As far as we are able, we have demonstrated the manner of the Instructor's love of humanity and his pedagogy. He has beautifully depicted himself as a "grain of mustard seed" (Matt 13:31), indicating the spiritual and fecund nature of the Word that is sown, and the magnificence and opulent growth latent in the Word's potency. With the seed's bitter taste he hints at the

11. *Gnōsis* here as elsewhere in his writings is Clement's choice term for the spiritual knowledge gained by maturing in the contemplation of God and the performance of virtue. Many other Greek patristic and monastic authors use it in this sense.

pungent and yet purgative benefit of the Word's censure. Given the allegorical polyvalence of the tiny grain, he grants salvation to all humanity. . . .

4.2 Origen, *Letter to Gregory Thaumaturgus*[12]

Greetings in God, from Origen to my good lord and most reverend son, Gregory. Natural ability, as you know, if properly trained, may be of the utmost possible service in promoting what I may call the "object" of human training. You, for instance, have ability enough to make you an expert in Roman law, or a philosopher in one of the Greek schools held in high esteem. I should like you, however, to make Christianity your "object," and to bring the whole force of your ability to bear upon it, with good effect. I am therefore very desirous that you should accept such parts even of Greek philosophy as may serve for the ordinary elementary instruction of our schools, and be a kind of preparation for Christianity; also those portions of geometry and astronomy likely to be of use in the interpretation of the sacred Scriptures, so that, what the pupils of the philosophers say about geometry and music, grammar, rhetoric, and astronomy, namely that they are the handmaidens of philosophy, we may say of philosophy itself in relation to Christianity.

Perhaps something of the kind is hinted at in the command from the mouth of God himself that the children of Israel be told to ask their neighbors and companions for vessels of silver and gold (Exod 11:2; 12:35–36) and for clothing, so that by spoiling the Egyptians they might find materials to make the things of which they were told (cf. Exod 25:40) for the divine service. For out of the spoils which the children of Israel took from the Egyptians came the contents of the Holy of Holies, the ark with its cover, and the Cherubim, and the mercy-seat, and the golden pot wherein was treasured up the manna, the Angels' bread. . . .

Why need I digress further to show how useful the things brought from Egypt were to the children of Israel, things which

---

12. Excerpted by Basil of Caesarea and Gregory of Nazianzus in *The Philokalia of Origen* 13, translated by George Lewis (Edinburgh: T&T Clark, 1911), 57–60. Revised and updated.

the Egyptians did not use properly, but the Hebrews through the wisdom of God turned to godly purposes? Divine Scripture knows, however, that some were the worse for the going down of the children of Israel from their own land into Egypt, and darkly hints that some do lose by sojourning with the Egyptians, that is to say, by lingering in the learning of the world after being nourished in the law of God and the divine worship of Israel. At all events, Hadad the Edomite (1 Kgs 11:14–22), so long as he was in the land of Israel, and did not taste the Egyptian bread, made no idols; but when he ran away from wise Solomon and went down into Egypt, running away one might say from the wisdom of God, he became Pharaoh's kinsman by marrying Pharaoh's wife's sister, and begetting a son brought up with Pharaoh's sons. And so it happened that although he returned into the land of Israel, he returned to divide God's people into two parts, and make them say over the golden calf, "These be thy Gods, O Israel, which brought thee up out of the land of Egypt" (1 Kgs 12:28). . . .

My lord and my son, chiefly give heed to the reading of the divine Scriptures; do give heed. For we need great attention when we read the divine writings, that we may not speak or form notions about them rashly. And as you give heed to reading the divine volume with a faithful anticipation well pleasing to God, knock at its closed doors and it shall be opened unto you by the porter, of whom Jesus said, "To him the porter opens" (John 10:3). And as you give heed to the divine reading, seek, in the right way and with an unfaltering faith in God, the meaning of the divine writings, which is hidden from the many. Be not content, however, with *knocking* and *seeking*; for prayer is the most necessary qualification for the understanding of divine things, and the Savior urged us to this when he said, not only, "Knock and it shall be opened, Seek and ye shall find" but also, "Ask and it shall be given unto you" (Matt 7:7). I have ventured thus far in my fatherly love for you; if I have done well or not in venturing, God and his Christ, and he that partakes of the Spirit of God and of the Spirit of Christ, alone can know. May you be a partaker, and ever increase the participation, that you say not only, "We have become partakers of Christ" (cf. Heb 3:14), but also, "We have become partakers of God" (cf. 2 Pet 1:4).

4.3 Gregory Thaumaturgus, *Panegyric on Origen*[13]

7. Surveying us, as it were, with a farmer's skill, and gauging us thoroughly, and not confining his notice to those things only which are obvious to everyone, and which are looked upon in open light, but penetrating into us more deeply, and probing what is most inward in us, he put us to the question, and made propositions to us, and listened to us in our replies; and whenever he thereby detected anything in us not wholly fruitless and profitless and waste, he set about clearing the soil, and turning it up and irrigating it, and putting all things in movement, and brought his whole skill and care to bear on us, and wrought upon our mind. And thorns and thistles, and every kind of wild herb or plant which our mind (so unregulated and precipitate in its own action) yielded and produced in its uncultured luxuriance and native wildness, he cut out and thoroughly removed by the processes of refutation and prohibition; sometimes assailing us in the genuine Socratic fashion, and again upsetting us by his argumentation whenever he saw us getting restive under him, like so many unbroken steeds, and springing out of the course and galloping madly about at random, until with a strange kind of persuasiveness and constraint he reduced us to a state of quietude under him by his discourse, which acted like a bridle in our mouth. And that was at first an unpleasant position for us, and one not without pain, as he dealt with persons who were unused to it, and still all untrained to submit to reason, when he plied us with his argumentations; and yet he purged us by them. And when he had made us adaptable, and had prepared us successfully for the reception of the words of truth, then, further, as though we were now a soil well-tilled and soft, and ready to impart growth to the seeds cast into it, he dealt liberally with us, and sowed the good seed in season, and attended to all the

---

13. Translated by S. D. F. Salmond, *Gregory Thaumaturgus, Dionysius the Great, Julius Africanus [et al.]*, Ante-Nicene Fathers, vol. 6 (Edinburgh: T&T Clark, 1885), 29, 30–31. Revised and updated.

other cares of good farming, each in its own proper season. And whenever he perceived any element of infirmity or baseness in our mind (whether it was of that character by nature, or had become thus gross through the excessive nurture of the body), he pricked it with his discourses, and reduced it by those delicate words and turns of reasoning which, although at first the very simplest, are gradually evolved one after the other, and skillfully wrought out, until they advance to a sort of complexity which can scarce be mastered or unfolded, and which cause us to start up, as it were, out of sleep. . . .

8. Nor did he confine his efforts merely to that form of the mind which it is the lot of dialectics to regulate; but he also took in hand that humble capacity of mind (which shows itself) in our amazement at the magnitude, and the wondrousness, and the magnificent and absolutely wise construction of the world, and in our marveling in a reasonless way, and in our being overpowered with fear, and in our knowing not, like the irrational creatures, what conclusion to come to. That, too, he aroused and corrected by other studies in natural science, illustrating and distinguishing the various divisions of created objects, and with admirable clearness reducing them to their pristine elements, taking them all up perspicuously in his discourse, and going over the nature of the whole, and of each several section, and discussing the multiform revolution and mutation of things in the world, until he carried us fully along with him under his clear teaching; and by those reasonings which he had partly learned from others, and partly found out for himself, he filled our minds with a rational instead of an irrational wonder at the sacred economy of the universe, and irreproachable constitution of all things. This is that sublime and heavenly study which is taught by natural philosophy[14]—a science most attractive to all. . . .

14. "Natural philosophy," or "physics," was less the observation of natural phenomena for their own sake than the study and contemplation of the natural order of creation for purposes of moral and religious edification. In the prologue to his *Commentary on the Song of Songs*, Origen situated "physics" in a three-fold curriculum between "ethics" proper and "epoptics," or metaphysical and theological mysteries. Interestingly, in conjunction with Old Testament Wisdom literature, Origen correlated ethics with Proverbs, physics with Ecclesiastes, and epoptics with the deeply mystical Song of Songs. This same "curriculum" appears in other late ancient Chris-

9. Moreover, as to those things which excel all in importance, and those for the sake of which, above all else, the whole family of the philosophical labors, gathering them like good fruits produced by the varied growths of all the other studies, and of long practiced philosophizing—I mean the divine virtues that concern the moral nature, by which the impulses of the mind have their equable and stable subsistence—through these, too, he aimed at making us truly proof against grief and disquietude under the pressure of all ills, and at imparting to us a well-disciplined and steadfast and religious spirit, so that we might be in all things truly blessed. And this he toiled at effecting by pertinent discourses, of a wise and soothing tendency, and very often also by the most cogent addresses touching our moral dispositions, and our modes of life. Nor was it only by words, but also by deeds, that he regulated in some measure our inclinations—namely, by that very contemplation and observation of the impulses and affections of the mind, by the issue of which most especially the mind is wont to be reduced to a right estate from one of discord, and to be restored to a condition of judgment and order out of one of confusion. . . .

4.4 Basil of Caesarea, *Address to Young Men on the Right Use of Greek Literature*[15]

Almost all who have written upon the subject of wisdom have more or less, in proportion to their several abilities, extolled virtue in their writings. Such men must one obey, and must try to realize their words in his life. For he, who by his works exemplifies the wisdom which with others is a matter of theory alone, "breathes; all others flutter about like shadows."[16] I think it is as if a painter should represent some marvel of manly beauty, and the subject should actually be such a man as the artist pictures on the canvas. To praise virtue in public with brilliant words and with

---

tian writers too, including Basil of Caesarea, Evagrius of Pontus, Jerome, and Olympiodorus of Alexandria.

15. Translated by Frederick Padelford, *Essays on the Study and Use of Poetry by Plutarch and Basil the Great* (New York: Holt, 1902), 108–11. Revised and updated.

16. Homer, *Odyssey* 10, l. 495.

long drawn-out speeches, while in private preferring pleasures to temperance, and self-interest to justice, finds an analogy on the stage, for the players frequently appear as kings and rulers, though they are neither, nor perhaps even genuinely free men. A musician would hardly put up with a lyre which was out of tune, nor a choregus with a chorus not singing in perfect harmony. But every man is divided against himself who does not make his life conform to his words, but who says with Euripides, "The mouth indeed hath sworn, but the heart knows no oath."[17] Such a man will seek the appearance of virtue rather than the reality. But to seem to be good when one is not so, is, if we are to respect the opinion of Plato at all,[18] the very height of injustice.

In this way, then, are we to receive those words from the pagan authors which contain suggestions of the virtues. But since also the renowned deeds of the men of old either are preserved for us by tradition, or are cherished in the pages of poet or historian, we must not fail to profit by them. A fellow of the street rabble once kept taunting Pericles, but he, meanwhile, gave no heed; and they held out all day, the fellow deluging him with reproaches, but he, for his part, not caring. Then when it was evening and dusk, and the fellow still clung to him, Pericles escorted him with a light, in order that he might not fail in the practice of philosophy.[19] Again, a man in a passion threatened and vowed death to Euclid of Megara,[20] but he in turn vowed that the man should surely be appeased, and cease from his hostility to him.

How invaluable it is to have such examples in mind when one is seized with anger! On the other hand, one must altogether ignore the tragedy which says in so many words: "Anger arms the hand against the enemy";[21] for it is much better not to give way to anger at all. But if such restraint is not easy, we shall at least curb our anger by reflection, so as not to give it too much rein.

17. *Hippolytus* l. 695.
18. See *Republic* 2, 361A.
19. See Plutarch, *Life of Pericles* 5.
20. See Plutarch, *Concerning the Cure of Anger* 14.
21. An ostensibly misquoted line from Euripides.

But let us bring our discussion back again to the examples of noble deeds. A certain man once kept striking Socrates, the son of Sophroniscus, in the face, yet he did not resent it, but allowed full play to the bully's anger, so that his face was swollen and bruised from the blows. Then when he stopped striking him, Socrates did nothing more than write on his forehead, as an artisan on a statue . . . and thus took out his revenge. Since these examples almost coincide with our teachings, I hold that such men are worthy of emulation. For this conduct of Socrates is akin to the precept that to the one who strikes you upon the one cheek, you should turn the other also (Matt 5:39)—thus much may you be avenged; the conduct of Pericles and of Euclid also conforms to the precept: "Submit to those who persecute you, and endure their wrath with meekness"; and to the other: "Pray for your enemies and curse them not" (Matt 5:44). One who has been instructed in the pagan examples will no longer hold the Christian precepts impracticable. But I will not overlook the conduct of Alexander, who, on taking captive the daughters of Darius, who were reputed to be of surpassing beauty, would not even look at them, for he deemed it unworthy of one who was a conqueror of men to be a slave to women.[22] This is of a piece with the statement that he who looks upon a woman to lust after her, even though he does not commit the act of adultery, is not free from its guilt, since he has entertained impure thoughts (Matt 5:28). It is hard to believe that the action of Cleinias, one of the disciples of Pythagoras, was in accidental conformity to our teachings, and not designed imitation of them. What, then, was this act of his? By taking an oath he could have avoided a fine of three talents, yet rather than do so he paid the fine, though he could have sworn truthfully. I am inclined to think that he had heard of the precept which forbids us to swear (cf. Lev 19:12; Deut 5:2).

---

22. See Plutarch, *Of the Fortune or Virtue of Alexander the Great* 2.6, 11.

4.5 Gregory of Nyssa: Reflections on His Sister Macrina as a Teacher of *Philosophia*

4.5.1 *Life of Macrina*[23]

Seeing as there was no longer any reason for them to continue their more or less materially-oriented life, Macrina convinced her mother to relinquish her customary life, with its ostentation and maidservants, to which she had grown accustomed for so long, in order to render her slaves and underlings sisters and equals in honor. . . .

So once attention to childrearing and concern for getting the children educated and established had ended for her mother, and most of the resources for material needs were divided up for the children, then, as I already mentioned, the life of the virgin Macrina became her mother's guide to this philosophical and immaterial way of life, turning her from everything that was habitual for her and introducing her to her own standard of humility. Macrina prepared her mother to become of equal honor with the whole company of virgins, such that she shared equally with them the same table, sleeping quarters, and all other necessities of life, and there was no disparity of worthiness between her life and theirs. The organization of their life, the high stature of their *philosophia*, the holy manner of their life in its daily and nightly regimen were such as exceed description in words. Just as, through death, souls are liberated from bodies and loosed from the concerns of mundane life, so their life together was separated from those things, resettled away from all worldly vanity, and trained to imitation of the angelic life. Among themselves they showed no anger, envy, hatred, contempt, or anything along those lines. Nor did they manifest desire for vanities like honor and glory, pride and arrogance; all such things they had rejected. . . . Rather, their sole concern was for divine realities accompanied by relentless prayer and continuous hymn-singing scheduled evenly throughout the day and

---

23. Translated from the Greek text edited by Virginia Callahan, *Opera Ascetica*, Gregorii Nysseni Opera, vol. 8, pt. 1 (Leiden: Brill, 1963), 377–78, 381–82.

night, so that these were at once their work and their rest from work. What human words could possibly bring such a life as this under review? For theirs was a life on the borderland between human and incorporeal nature. . . .

4.5.2 Dialogue on the Soul and Resurrection[24]

When Basil, much esteemed among the saints, departed human life to be with God, and a common occasion for sorrow came over the churches, my sister and teacher [Macrina] was still alive and I hastened to share with her what had happened to our brother. My soul was full of pain as I grieved exceedingly at such a huge loss, and so I pursued someone with whom to share my tears, my equal in bearing the burden of grief. When we were together face to face, the sight of my teacher moved me to emotion, for she was already sick and approaching death. But like those who know how to tame horses, she allowed me to be carried away for a while by the torrent of my emotion, and after that tried verbally to harness me, as if reining in the disorder of my soul with the bridle of her own reasoning. She cited the apostolic dictum:

Macrina: "It is not necessary to grieve for those who have fallen asleep, for this passion belongs only to those who have no hope" (cf. 1 Thess 4:13).

Gregory: My heart still raging with grief, I asked her, "How is this to be accomplished by human beings when each of us has a natural aversion to death and none of us easily manages the sight of those who are dying, and even the dying try to flee when death approaches? . . . But we also see that all human diligence dwells on this one thing: how to remain alive . . ."

Macrina: My teacher then asked, "What is it about death itself that appears so exceedingly grievous to you? Surely the habitual

---

24. Translated from the Greek text edited by Andreas Spira and Ekkehard Mühlenberg, *Gregorii Nysseni de anima et resurrectione*, Gregorii Nysseni Opera, vol. 3, pt. 3 (Leiden: Brill, 2014), 1–3, 4.

view of death among irrational people is not sufficient to make you repudiate it!"

Gregory: "Is it not worthy of grief," I said to her, "when we see one who was recently alive and talking suddenly void of breath, speech, or motion, all their physical senses gone, having no vision, no hearing, nor any other faculty used for perception? . . ."

Macrina: She said, "Is not what troubles and constrains your mind the fear that the soul does not endure forever, but comes to an end with the dissolution of the body? . . ."

4.6 Gregory of Nazianzus, *Oration 16 (On His Father's Silence on Account of the Plague of Hail)*[25]

2. I have not yet alluded to the true and first wisdom, for which our wonderful farmer and shepherd is conspicuous.[26] The first wisdom is a life worthy of praise, and kept pure for God, or being purified for him who is all-pure and all-luminous, who demands of us, us his only sacrifice, purification—that is, a contrite heart and the sacrifice of praise (Heb 13:15) and a new creation in Christ (2 Cor 5:17) and the new man (Eph 4:24), and the like, as the Scripture loves to call it. The first wisdom is to despise that wisdom which consists of language and figures of speech, and spurious and unnecessary embellishments. Be it mine to speak five words with my understanding in the Church, rather than ten thousand words in an [ecstatic] tongue (1 Cor 14:19), and with the unmeaning voice of a trumpet (1 Cor 14:8), which does not rouse my soldier to the spiritual combat. This is the wisdom which I praise, which I welcome. By this the igno-

---

25. Translated by Charles Browne and James Swallow, *Cyril of Jerusalem, Gregory Nazianzen*, Nicene and Post-Nicene Fathers, 2nd series, vol. 7 (Edinburgh: T&T Clark, 1894), 247–48, 248–49, 250, 253. Revised and updated.

26. Gregory here is defending his father and predecessor Gregory the Elder, who, as bishop of Nazianzus, remained dumbstruck before his congregation in the wake of a disastrous hailstorm, but whose pastoral integrity and goodness were already proven. The son must now compensate for his father's silence, and he begins by downplaying the role of mere rhetoric as a source of wisdom—a good excuse for his father's reticence to speak about the crisis.

ble have won renown, and the despised have attained the highest honors. By this a crew of fishermen have taken the whole world in the meshes of the Gospel-net, and overcome by a word finished and cut short (cf. Isa 10:22–23 LXX; Rom 9:28) the wisdom that comes to naught (1 Cor 2:6). I count not wise the one who is clever in words, nor the one who is of a ready tongue, but unstable and undisciplined in soul, like the tombs which, fair and beautiful as they are outwardly, are fetid with corpses within (cf. Matt 23:27), and full of manifold foul smells; but rather him who speaks but little of virtue, yet gives many examples of it in his practice, and proves the trustworthiness of his language by his life.

3. Fairer in my eyes, is the beauty which we can gaze upon than that which is painted in words: of more value the wealth which our hands can hold, than that which is imagined in our dreams; and more real the wisdom of which we are convinced by deeds, than that which is set forth in splendid language. For "a good understanding," says the Psalmist, "is for those who practice it" (Ps 110:10 LXX; Ps 111:10 Hebrew), not those who merely preach it. Time is the best touchstone of this wisdom, and "old age is a crown of glory" (Prov 16:31). . . .

4. Tell us where such blows and scourges come from, and what account we can give of them. Is it some disordered and irregular motion or some unguided current, some unreason of the universe, as though there were no Ruler of the world, which is therefore borne along by chance, as is the doctrine of the foolishly wise, who are themselves borne along at random by the disorderly spirit of darkness? Or are the disturbances and changes of the universe—which was originally constituted, blended, bound together, and set in motion in a harmony known only to him who gave it motion—directed by reason and order under the guidance of the reins of Providence? Where do famines and tornadoes and hailstorms, our present warning blow, come from? Where do pestilences, diseases, earthquakes, tidal waves, and fearful things in the heavens come from? And how is the creation, once ordered for the enjoyment of human beings, as their common and equal delight, changed for the

punishment of the ungodly, in order that we may be chastised through that for which, when honored with it, we did not give thanks, and recognize in our sufferings that power which we did not recognize in our benefits? How is it that some receive at the Lord's hand double for their sins (Isa 40:2), and the measure of their wickedness is doubly filled up, as in the correction of Israel, while the sins of others are done away by a sevenfold recompense into their bosom (Ps 79:12)? . . .

5. Terrible is an unfruitful season, and the loss of the crops. It could not be otherwise, when people are already rejoicing in their hopes, and counting on their all but harvested stores. Terrible again is an unseasonable harvest, when the farmers labor with heavy hearts, sitting as it were beside the grave of their crops, which the gentle rain nourished, but the wild storm has rooted up, whereof the mower fills not his hand, neither he that binds up the sheaves his bosom (Ps 129:7) nor have they obtained the blessing which passers-by bestow upon the farmers. Wretched indeed is the sight of the ground devastated, cleared, and shorn of its ornaments. . . .

6. What shall we do in the day of visitation (Isa 10:3) with which one of the prophets terrifies me, whether that of the righteous sentence of God against us, or that upon the mountains and hills, of which we have heard, or whatever and whenever it may be, when he will reason with us, and oppose us, and set before us those bitter accusers (cf. Ps 50:21), our sins, comparing our wrongdoings with our benefits, and striking thought with thought, and scrutinizing action with action, and calling us to account for the image (Gen 1:26) which has been blurred and spoiled by wickedness, till at last he leads us away self-convicted and self-condemned, no longer able to say that we are being unjustly treated—a thought which is able even here sometimes to console in their condemnation those who are suffering. . . .

17. Only let us recognize the purpose of the evil. Why have the crops withered, our storehouses been emptied, the pastures of our flocks failed, the fruits of the earth been withheld, and the plains been filled with shame instead of with fatness? Why have

valleys lamented and not abounded in corn, the mountains not dropped sweetness, as they shall do hereafter to the righteous, but been stripped and dishonored, and received on the contrary the curse of Gilboa (2 Sam 1:21)? The whole earth has become as it was in the beginning, before it was adorned with its beauties. "You visited the earth, and made it to drink" (Ps 65:9)—but the visitation has been for evil, and the drink destructive. Alas! What a spectacle! Our prolific crops reduced to stubble, the seed we sowed is recognized by scanty remains, and our harvest, the approach of which we reckon from the number of the months, instead of from the ripening corn, scarcely bears the first-fruits for the Lord. Such is the wealth of the ungodly, such the harvest of the careless sower; as the ancient curse runs, to look for much, and bring in little (Hag 1:9), to sow and not reap, to plant and not press (Deut 28:39), ten acres of vineyard to yield one bath (Isa 5:10); and to hear of fertile harvests in other lands, and be ourselves pressed by famine. Why this, and what is the cause of the breach? Let us not wait to be convicted by others, let us be our own examiners. . . .

18. One of us has oppressed the poor, and wrested from him his portion of land, and wrongly encroached upon his landmark by fraud or violence, and joined house to house, and field to field, to rob his neighbor of something, and been eager to have no neighbor, so as to dwell alone on the earth (Isa 5:8). Another has defiled the land with usury and interest, both gathering where he had not sowed and reaping where he had not strawed (cf. Matt 25:26), farming, not the land, but the necessity of the needy. Another has robbed God (Mal 3:8), the giver of all, of the first-fruits of the barn floor and winepress, showing himself at once thankless and senseless, in neither giving thanks for what he has had, nor prudently providing, at least, for the future. Another has had no pity on the widow and orphan, and not imparted his bread and meagre nourishment to the needy, or rather to Christ, who is nourished in the persons of those who are nourished even in a slight degree; a man perhaps of much property unexpectedly gained, for this is the most unjust of all, who finds his many barns too narrow for him, filling some and emptying others, to build greater ones for future crops

(cf. Luke 12:18), not knowing that he is being snatched away with hopes unrealized, to give an account of his riches and fancies, and proved to have been a bad steward of another's goods. Another has turned aside the way of the meek (Amos 2:7), and turned aside the just among the unjust; another has hated him that reproves in the gates (Isa 29:21), and abhorred him who speaks uprightly (Amos 5:10); another has sacrificed to his net which catches much (Hab 1:16), and keeping the spoil of the poor in his house (Isa 3:14), has either remembered not God, or remembered him ill—by saying "Blessed be the Lord, for we are rich" (Zech 11:5), and wickedly supposed that he received these things from him by whom he will be punished. For because of these things cometh the wrath of God upon the children of disobedience (Eph 5:6). Because of these things the heaven is shut, or opened for our punishment; and much more, if we do not repent, even when smitten, and draw near to him who approaches us through the powers of nature....

4.7 Ephrem the Syrian, *Hymn on Paradise* 3 (Stanzas 1–7)[27]

1. As for that part of the Garden, my beloved,
    which is situated so gloriously
 at the summit of that height
    where dwells the Glory,
 not even its symbol
    can be depicted in man's thought;
 for what mind
    has the sensitivity
 to gaze upon it,
    or the faculties to explore it,
 or the capacity to attain to that Garden
    whose riches are beyond comprehension.
 Response: *Praise to Your Justice that crowns the victorious.*

---

27. Translated by Sebastian Brock, *St. Ephrem the Syrian: Hymns on Paradise*, Popular Patristics Series, vol. 10 (Crestwood, NY: St. Vladimir's Seminary Press, 1990), 90–93. Reprinted by permission of St. Vladimir's Seminary Press.

2. Perhaps that blessed tree,
      the Tree of Life,
   is, by its rays,
      the sun of Paradise;
   its leaves glisten,
      and on them are impressed
   the spiritual graces
      of the Garden.
   In the breezes the other trees
      bow down as if in worship
   before that sovereign
      and leader of the trees.
   Response: *Praise to Your Justice that crowns the victorious.*

3. In the midst He planted
      the Tree of Knowledge (Gen 2:9),
   endowing it with awe,
      hedging it in with dread,
   so that it might straightaway serve
      as a boundary to the inner region of Paradise.
   Two things did Adam hear
      in that single decree:
   that they should not eat of it (Gen 2:17)
      and that, by shrinking from it,
   they should perceive that it was not lawful
      to penetrate further, beyond that Tree (Gen 3:7).
   Response: *Praise to Your Justice that crowns the victorious.*

4. The serpent could not
      enter Paradise,
   for neither animal
      nor bird
   was permitted to approach
      the outer region of Paradise,
   and Adam had to go out
      to meet them;
   so the serpent cunningly learned,

through questioning Eve,
the character of Paradise,
what it was and how it was ordered.

5. When the accursed one learned
how the glory of that inner Tabernacle,
as if in a sanctuary,
was hidden from them,
and that the Tree of Knowledge,
clothed with an injunction,
served as the veil
for the sanctuary,
he realized that its fruit
was the key of justice
that would open the eyes of the bold
—and cause them great remorse.
Response: *Praise to Your Justice that crowns the victorious.*

6. Their eyes were open—
though at the same time they were still closed
so as not to see the Glory
or their own low estate,
so as not to see the Glory
of that inner Tabernacle,
nor to see the nakedness of their own bodies.
These two kinds of knowledge
God hid in the Tree,
placing it as a judge between the two parties.
Response: *Praise to Your Justice that crowns the victorious.*

7. But when Adam boldly ran
and ate of its fruit
this double knowledge
straight away flew toward him,
tore away and removed
both veils from his eyes:
he beheld the Glory of the Holy of Holies

and trembled;
he beheld, too, his own shame and blushed,
    groaning and lamenting
because the twofold knowledge he had gained
had proved for him a torment.
Response: *Praise to Your Justice that crowns the victorious.*

4.8 Augustine, *On the Trinity*, Book 13[28]

13.19.24. And all these things which the Word-made-flesh did and suffered for us in time and place belong, according to the distinction which we have undertaken to demonstrate, to knowledge, not to wisdom. And as the Word is without time and without place, he is co-eternal with the Father, and in his wholeness everywhere; and if anyone can, and as much as he can, speak truly concerning this Word, then his discourse will pertain to wisdom. And hence the Word-made-flesh, which is Christ Jesus, has the treasures both of wisdom and of knowledge. For the Apostle, writing to the Colossians, says: "For I want you to know what great struggle I am having for you, and for those at Laodicea, and for as many as have not seen my face in the flesh; that their hearts might be comforted, being knit together in love, and unto all riches of the full assurance of understanding, to the acknowledgment of the mystery of God which is Christ Jesus: in whom are hid all the treasures of wisdom and knowledge" (Col 2:1–3). To what extent the Apostle knew all those treasures, how much of them he had penetrated, and to what great things he had reached, who can know? Yet, for my part, according to that which is written, "But the manifestation of the Spirit is given to everyone for profit; for to one is given by the Spirit the word of wisdom, to another the word of knowledge by the same Spirit" (1 Cor 12:7–8). If these two are accordingly to be distinguished from each other, that wisdom is to be assigned to divine things, knowledge to human, then I acknowledge both in Christ, and so with me do all his faithful ones. And

---

28. Translated by Arthur Haddan and William Shedd, *On the Holy Trinity, Doctrinal Treatises, Moral Treatises*, Nicene and Post-Nicene Fathers, 1st series, vol. 3 (Edinburgh: T&T Clark, 1873), 180–81. Revised and updated.

when I read, "The Word was made flesh, and dwelt among us," I understand by the Word the true Son of God, I acknowledge in the flesh the true Son of Man, and both together joined into one Person of God and humanity, by an ineffable copiousness of grace. And on account of this, the Apostle goes on to say, "And we beheld His glory, the glory as of the Only-begotten of the Father, full of grace and truth" (John 1:14). If we refer grace to knowledge, and truth to wisdom, I think we shall not swerve from that distinction between these two things which we have commended. For in those things that have their origin in time, this is the highest grace, that man is joined with God in unity of person; but in things eternal the highest truth is rightly attributed to the Word of God. But that the same is himself the Only-Begotten of the Father, full of grace and truth—this took place, in order that he himself in things done for us in time should be the same for whom we are cleansed by the same faith, that we may contemplate him steadfastly in things eternal. And those distinguished philosophers of the heathen who have been able to understand and discern the invisible things of God by those things which are made, have yet, as is said of them, "held down the truth in iniquity" (Rom 1:23); because they philosophized without a Mediator, that is, without the man Christ, whom they neither believed to be about to come at the word of the prophets, nor to have come at that of the apostles. For, placed as they were in these lowest things, they could not but seek some media through which they might attain to those lofty things which they had understood; and so they fell upon deceitful spirits, through whom it came to pass, that "they changed the glory of the incorruptible God into an image made like to corruptible man, and to birds, and four-footed beasts, and creeping things" (Rom 1:18, 23). For in such forms also they set up or worshipped idols. Therefore Christ is our knowledge, and the same Christ is also our wisdom. He himself implants in us faith concerning temporal things; he himself shows forth the truth concerning eternal things. Through him we reach on to himself: we stretch through knowledge to wisdom; yet we do not withdraw from one and the same Christ, "in whom are hidden all the treasures of wisdom and of knowledge."[29] But now we speak of knowledge, and will hereafter speak of wisdom as much as he himself shall grant.

---

29. On Christ as divine Wisdom incarnate, see also Augustine's *On Christian Doctrine* 1.11.11–1.14.13.

5.

Biblical Narrative, Hagiography, and Moral Mimesis

INTRODUCTION

To a significant extent, early Christians read the Bible as a panorama of narratives of all kinds, many of which carried multiple meanings for the church. Some biblical narratives were understood to have been recorded clearly or literally for moral or religious edification, like the story of Job, a righteous believer severely tested by God—although even Job was rendered typologically as a Christ-figure by some interpreters. Other biblical narratives, however, seemed to have much more latent moral or spiritual lessons, requiring greater interpretive excavation; and still other stories were perceived to be overtly "scandalous," as Origen said, because their details appeared objectionable or detrimental to the coherence of Scripture.[1] Origen famously reasoned that these *skandala* were deliberately inserted in Scripture by the divine author as goads against interpretive laziness. Origen and his many later devotees insisted these troublesome texts could still be rich in figurative or allegorical senses, the kinds of

---

1. For his teaching on biblical *skandala*, see Origen's *On First Principles* 4.2.8–4.3.15.

meaning that were the reward of diligently searching the texts beyond their literal or superficial sense.

Origen furthermore proved to be a master of interpretive mimesis, of *re*-presenting the significance of a biblical narrative within the "higher" register of God's revelatory economy centered climactically in Jesus Christ. The short excerpt from Origen's fourth *Homily on Joshua* [5.1] is a splendid example and there are many others in his preaching. From the Israelites' exodus across the Red Sea, the events at Sinai, and the crossing of the Jordan River into the promised land, he envisioned an elaborate and elegant typology of the mystery of baptism and of the moral and spiritual conversion of the believer or catechumen. Using a similar interpretive mimesis, Ambrose of Milan, being a great admirer of Origen's exegesis, employed hermeneutically simple typologies of biblical saints to construct models of the moral and spiritual life of the Christian. In his *On the Duties of the Clergy* [5.2], a work in part modeled after the *De Officiis* of Cicero, Ambrose furnished Christian exemplars of the four cardinal virtues of pagan moral tradition. Though he often mixed and matched these virtues among the great biblical saints, Ambrose saw Abraham especially as embodying prudence, Moses and Elisha justice, Job fortitude, and David temperance. Ambrose intended the clergy to become, in their turn, exemplars of these same virtues for the laity.

Basil of Caesarea's *Homily on the Forty Martyrs of Sebaste* [5.3], a group of Christian soldiers in Armenia who lost their lives for refusing to sacrifice to pagan deities, vividly demonstrates the kind of preaching that attended the growing cult of the martyrs and saints in the fourth century and beyond. Basil uses rhetorical *ekphrasis*, graphic depiction, both to amplify the drama of the saints' demise and bolster his recommendation of their imitable endurance and faithfulness to his church audience.

I have included the passage from the anonymous Syriac *Life of Abraham of Qidun* [5.4] as beautifully exhibiting both interpretive and moral mimesis in late ancient hagiography. The story is not biblical, but like many such hagiographical texts, it includes clear mimetic resonances of characters and episodes in Scripture. The hero here, a fourth-century recluse, had taken custody of his orphaned niece, Mary, and raised her for the ascetical life until she fell into prostitution. Abraham appears as something of an "incarnational" Christ-figure when he pursues the young woman (herself mirroring the prodigal son or the lost sheep of Luke 15), disguising himself in a soldier's garb as a prospective lover in order, by an opportune intimacy, to recall Mary to her true self. The story solicits imitation not only of Abraham's selflessness and mercy but Mary's profound compunction and tears. Indeed, it is a narrative of repentance that might well have been included among the texts set out back in chapter 1.

Much early monastic literature is teeming with moral and spiritual exempla drawn from the Bible, and understandably so. The incipient *lectio divina* ("spiritual reading") of Scripture by monks entailed a relentless searching of the hidden depths of sacred revelation, but in the meantime, monks needed immediately accessible paragons of the ascetical virtues, to whom they could return again and again for inspiration. Indeed, many biblical saints were seen as proto-monks (Adam, Moses, Elijah, John the Baptist, et al.), and in the fourth-century monk Nilus of Ancyra's letter to Maximus the Presbyter [5.5], we find this mimetic pattern both defended and promoted. For Nilus, the Bible is a veritable gallery of exemplars of virtues and vices, and in the ascetical drama that is still unfolding in the present, persons spiritually resume the roles of ancient heroes and villains alike, depending on the orientation of their moral performances.

Gregory the Great, the monk-turned-Pope (r. 590–604), continued in this same vein. His *Moralia* is by far the longest commentary on the book of Job from Christian antiquity, and as the introductory letter to it indicates [5.6.1], he approached the book presupposing its multiple senses (viz. literal, moral, allegorical) and hoping to spell them out more or less systematically. Much of Gregory's commentary takes the traditional line that Job was a model of righteousness and patience, and largely circumvents the book's questioning of God's justice. I have chosen the particular passage here [5.6.2] because it deals with Job precisely in one of his most defiant moments, cursing the very day of his birth (Job 3:1–4). Was this pious behavior? In this instance too, Gregory does not see Job compromising his godliness, since he was not disparaging the fact that God created him but only condemning the morally debauched age after the Adamic fall in which all of us human beings find ourselves presently struggling.

THE TEXTS

5.1 Origen, *Homily 4 on Joshua*[2]

1. To a sinner, all creation is an enemy, just as it is written concerning the Egyptians: The land fought them, the air itself and the heavens fought them. But to the just person, even things that seem inaccessible are made plain and easy. The just person crosses the Red Sea as though on dry land, but if an Egyptian wishes to cross, he is overwhelmed, and no wall of water will be made for him on the right and on the left (cf. Exod 14:22, 29). Even if the just person enters a dreadful wilderness and wasteland, food is provided from the heavens (Exod 16:13–15; Ps 78:24).

Thus in the Jordan, the ark of the covenant was the leader for the people of God. The order of priests and Levites stand together, and the waters, as though signifying a certain respect, hold back their course for the ministers of God and are heaped up together into a mass, yielding a harmless journey for the people of God (Josh 3:15–17).

Lest you marvel when these deeds concerning the former people are applied to you, O Christian, the divine word promises much greater and loftier things for you who, through the sacrament of baptism, have parted the waters of the Jordan. It promises a way and a passage for you through the air itself. Indeed, hear what Paul says concerning just persons: "We," he says, "shall be seized up into the clouds to meet Christ in the air and thus shall always be with the Lord" (1 Thess 4:17). There is nothing at all that the just one should fear. All creation waits upon that person. Hear, finally, how God makes this promise even through the prophet, saying to him, "If you pass through

---

2. Translated by Barbara Bruce, Fathers of the Church, vol. 105 (Washington, DC: Catholic University of America Press, 2002), 51–53. Reprinted by permission of the Catholic University of America Press.

the fire, the flame will not hurt you, because I am the Lord your God" (Isa 43:2–3). Therefore each place receives the just one, and all creation renders a servitude it owes.

And do not imagine that these deeds are only in former times and nothing so great as this is brought forth in you who are now the hearer of them. For all things are fulfilled in you according to a mystical reckoning.[3] Indeed you who long to draw near to the hearing of the divine law have recently forsaken the darkness of idolatry and are now for the first time forsaking Egypt. When you are reckoned among the number of catechumens and have undertaken to submit to the precepts of the Church, you have parted the Red Sea and, placed in the stations of the desert, you daily devote yourself to hearing the Law of God and to looking upon the face of Moses, through which the glory of the Lord is revealed. But if you also have entered the mystic font of baptism and in the presence of the priestly and Levitical order have been instructed by those venerable and magnificent sacraments, which are known to those who are permitted to know those things, then, with the Jordan parted, you will enter the land of promise by the services of the priests. In this land, Jesus receives you after Moses, and becomes for you the leader of a new way.

Mindful of such great and excellent powers of God—that the sea was divided for you and that the river's water stood upright—you will turn and say to it, "Why is it, O Sea, that you fled? And you, Jordan, that you turned backwards? Mountains, why did you skip about like rams, and the hills like lambs of the flock?" (Ps 114:5–6). But the divine word will respond to you and say, "By the face of the Lord is the land aroused, by the face of the God of Jacob who turns the rock into a pool of water and the cliff into springs of waters" (Ps 114:7–8). . . .

---

3. Cf. 1 Cor. 10:11, a text cherished by Origen in his moral and spiritual interpretation of Scripture.

5.2 Ambrose, *On the Duties of the Clergy*, Book 1[4]

1.24.105. Let us now consider what befits an active life. We note that there are three things to be regarded in connection with this subject. One is, that passion should not resist our reason. In that way only can our duties be brought into line with what is seemly. For if passion yields to reason we can easily maintain what is seemly in our duties. Next, we must take care lest, either by showing greater zeal or less than the matter we take up demands, we look as though we were taking up a small matter with great parade or were treating a great matter with but little care. Thirdly, as regards moderation in our endeavors and works, and also with regard to order in doing things and in the right timing of things, I think that everything should be open and straightforward.

1.24.106. But first comes that which I may call the foundation of all, namely, that our passions should obey our reason. The second and third are really the same—moderation in either case. There is room with us for the survey of a pleasing form, which is accounted beauty, and the consideration of dignity. Next follows the consideration of the order and the timing of things. These, then, are the three points, and we must see whether we can show them in perfection in any one of the saints.

1.24.107. First there is our father Abraham, who was formed and called for the instruction of generations to come (cf. Gen 12:1–4).[5] When bidden to go forth from his own country and kindred and from his father's house, though bound and held back by many ties of relationship, did he not give proof that in him passion was subject to reason? Who does not delight in

---

4. Translated by H. de Romestin, *Some of the Principal Works of St. Ambrose*, Nicene and Post-Nicene Fathers, 2nd series, vol. 10 (Edinburgh: T&T Clark, 1885), 18–20. Revised and updated.

5. Not only Abraham but the other Hebrew patriarchs as well were especially important moral exemplars in Ambrose's ethics, and not only here in this work for clergy but in his other exegetical-moral treatises on the patriarchs, which, as Marcia Colish has shown, sought to relate their moral virtues to the average Christian. See her *Ambrose's Patriarchs: Ethics for the Common Man* (Notre Dame, IN: University of Notre Dame Press, 2005).

the sweet charms of his native land, his kindred, and his own home? Their sweetness then delighted him. But the thought of the heavenly command and of an eternal reward influenced him more. Did he not reflect that he could not take his wife with him without the greatest danger, unused as she was to hardships, and so tender to bear insults, and so beautiful as to be likely to arouse the lust of profligate men? Yet he decided somewhat deliberately to undergo all this rather than to escape it by making excuses. Lastly, when he had gone into Egypt, he advised her to say she was his sister, not his wife (Gen 12:11–13).

1.24.108. See here what passions are at work! He feared for the chastity of his wife, he feared for his own safety, he had his suspicions about the lust of the Egyptians, and yet the reasonableness of performing his duty to God prevailed with him. For he thought that by the favor of God he could be safe everywhere, but if he offended the Lord he could not abide unharmed even at home. Thus reason conquered passion, and brought it into subjection to itself.

1.24.109. When his nephew was taken captive (Gen 14:14), without being terrified or dismayed at the hordes of so many kings, he resumed the war. And after the victory was gained he refused his share of the spoil, which he himself had really won. Also, when a son was promised him, though he thought of the lost vigor of his body, now as good as dead, and the barrenness of his wife, and his own great age, he believed God, though it was against the law of nature (Gen 15:4; 17:15).

1.24.110. Note how everything comes together here. Passion was not wanting, but it was checked. Here was a mind equable in action, which neither treated great things as unimportant or little things as great. Here there was moderation in different affairs, order in things, fitness of occasion, due measure in words. He was foremost in faith, conspicuous in virtue, vigorous in battle, in victory not greedy, at home hospitable, and to his wife attentive.

1.24.111. Jacob also, his holy grandson, loved to pass his time at home free from danger; but his mother wished him to live in foreign parts, and so to give place to his brother's anger (Gen 27:42). Sound counsels prevailed over natural feelings. An exile from home, banished from his parents, yet everywhere, in all he did, he observed due measure, such as was fitting, and made use of his opportunities at the right time. So dear was he to his parents at home, that the one, moved by the promptness of his compliance, gave him his blessing, the other inclined towards him with tender love. In the judgment of his brother, also, he was placed first, when he thought that he ought to give up his food to his brother (Gen 25:34). For though according to his natural inclinations he wished for food, yet when asked for it he gave it up from a feeling of brotherly affection. He was a faithful shepherd of the flock for his master, an attentive son-in-law to his father-in-law; he was active in work, sparing in his meals, conspicuous in making amends, lavish in repaying. So well, at last, did he calm his brother's anger that he received his favor, though he had feared his enmity (Gen 33:4).

1.24.112. What shall I say of Joseph? (Genesis 39). He certainly had a longing for freedom, and yet endured the bonds of servitude. How meek he was in slavery, how unchanging in virtue, how kindly in prison! Wise, too, in interpreting, and self-restrained in exercising his power! In the time of plenty was he not careful? In the time of famine was he not fair? Did he not praiseworthily do everything in order, and use opportunities at their season; giving justice to his people by the restraining guidance of his office?

1.24.113. Job also, both in prosperity and adversity, was blameless, patient, pleasing, and acceptable to God. He was harassed with pain, yet could find consolation.

1.24.114. David also was brave in war, patient in time of adversity, peaceful at Jerusalem, in the hour of victory merciful, on committing sin repentant, in his old age foreseeing. He preserved due measure in his actions, and took his opportunities as they came. He has set them down in the songs of succeeding years; and so it seems to me that he has by his life no less than by the sweetness of his hymns poured forth an undying song of his own merits to God.

1.24.115. What duty connected with the chief virtues was wanting in these men?[6] In the first place they showed *prudence*, which is exercised in the search of the truth, and which imparts a desire for full knowledge; next, *justice*, which assigns each man his own, does not claim another's, and disregards its own advantage, so as to guard the rights of all; thirdly, *fortitude*, which both in warfare and at home is conspicuous in greatness of mind and distinguishes itself in the strength of the body; fourthly, *temperance*, which preserves the right method and order in all things that we think should either be done or said.[7]

5.3 Basil of Caesarea, *Homily on the Forty Martyrs of Sebaste*[8]

2. Come, then, let us bring [the martyrs] into prominence by remembering them, let us present to those who are here the common benefit deriving from them, demonstrating to everyone, as if it were in writing, the acts of the men's prowess. When often both historians and painters express manly deeds of war, the one embellishing them with words, the other engraving them onto tablets, they both arouse many too to bravery. The facts which the historical account presents by being listened to, the painting silently portrays by imitation. In this very way let us too remind those present of the men's virtue, and as it were by bringing their deeds to their gaze, let us motivate them to imitate those who are nobler and closer to them with respect to the course of their life. I mean that this is the encomium of the martyrs: the exhortation of the congregation to virtue....

---

6. Cf. Cicero, *De officiis* 1.5.
7. Here Ambrose summarizes how these Old Testament heroes were exemplars of the four cardinal virtues already enshrined in pagan moral philosophy: *prudentia, justitia, fortitudo*, and *temperantia*.
8. Translated by Pauline Allen, *"Let Us Die That We May Live": Greek Homilies on Christian Martyrs from Asia Minor, Palestine and Syria c. 350-c. 450* (London: Routledge, 2003), 68–69, 70, 71–73, 75–76. Reprinted by permission of Routledge.

3. When that godless and impious edict was promulgated, to not confess Christ or to expect danger, every kind of punishment was threatened, and great and savage was the wrath aroused by the judges of iniquity against the pious.... Then those men, the invincible and noble soldiers of Christ, came into the public eye, while the official was displaying the emperor's instructions and demanding obedience. With forthright voice, they boldly and courageously declared themselves to be Christians, in no way cowering before what they saw, nor panic-stricken at what was threatened.

4. When that boastful and barbarous [official] heard this, not being able to bear the forthrightness of the men, he boiled over with rage, and considered finding some device to kill them both slowly and painfully at the same time. Finally he had an idea, and consider how cruel it was. For after looking around at the nature of the country, that it was icy-cold, and the season of the year, which was winter, and keeping a watch for the night on which the most harm could be extended, especially then when the north wind was blowing on it, he gave orders that everybody was to be stripped and to be made to freeze to death in the open air in the middle of the city....

5. So when they heard the order..., with great joy each of them threw off even the last tunic, and went to their death by cold, encouraging each other as if they were seizing spoils. "Let us not take off a garment," they said, "but let us 'put off the old man who has been corrupted through his desire for error' (Eph 4:22). Let us give thanks to you, Lord, as we cast off sin together with this garment. Since we put on clothes because of the snake (cf. Gen 3:21), let us take them off because of Christ. Let us not hold on to clothes because of the paradise which we have lost. What shall we give back to the Lord (Ps 115:3)? Our Lord also took his clothes off. What greater suffering can a slave have [than to] suffer what his Master did? I should say that we were the ones who took off the clothes of the Master himself (cf. Matt 27:28). I mean that this was that shameless act of soldiers—they took off his clothes and divided his garments (Matt 27:35). So let us delete the written charge against us by our own efforts. Win-

ter is piercing, but paradise is sweet. Freezing is painful, but rest is pleasing. Let us wait for a little while, and the bosom of the patriarch will comfort us. . . ."

Providing these encouraging words to each other, and each of them enjoining the other, as if they were fulfilling a guard's role in war, they passed the night, bearing the present circumstances nobly, rejoicing in what they hoped for, ridiculing the enemy. There was one prayer from all of them. "The forty of us went into the stadium; let the forty of us be crowned, Master. Let not even one person be missing from that number. It is an honorable [number], which you honored in your fast of forty days (cf. Matt 4:2), through which law-giving came into the world (cf. Exod 34:28). After a forty-day fast seeking the Lord, Elias had a vision (cf. 1 Kgs 19:8)."

7. And the one [soldier who betrayed the forty] who loved life fell, having transgressed in vain, while the public executioner, as he saw him give way and run to the baths, put himself in the place of the deserter, threw off his clothes and joined in with the naked men, shouting the same cry as the saints: "I am a Christian." And astounding those present with the swiftness of the change, he both filled the number, and by adding himself he softened the grief concerning the one who had lost his nerve, imitating those in the line of battle, who, when one man falls in the front line, immediately fill up the phalanx, so that the close battle order is not broken by the man's departure. He too did something similar. He saw the heavenly miracles, he recognized the truth, he sought refuge with the Master, he was numbered with the martyrs. He renewed the deeds of the disciples. Judas departed, and Matthias was substituted (cf. Acts 1:26). He became an imitator of Paul, the persecutor yesterday, today the evangelist (cf. Acts 9:1–30). He too had a call from above, "not from human beings, nor through a human being" (Gal 1:1). He believed in the name of our Lord Jesus Christ; he was baptized into him, not by another, but by his own faith, not in water, but in his own blood.

8. And so, as the day began, while they were still breathing they were delivered over to the fire, and the remains of the fire were

scattered on the river. As a result, the suffering of the blessed ones went completely through all creation. They suffered on earth, they remained steadfast in the air; they were delivered over to the fire; the water received them. Theirs was the saying: "We went through fire and water, and you have led us out into relief" (Ps 66:12). . . .

Bounteous benevolence, unsquandered grace, ready help for Christians, a church of martyrs, an army of torch-bearers, a chorus of those giving praise. . . .

O holy chorus! O hallowed battalion! O unbroken fighting order! O common guards of the human race! Good companions in times of anxiety, helpers in prayer, most powerful ambassadors, stars of the world, flowers of the churches. The earth does not hide you; instead, heaven accepts you. The gates of paradise have opened for you. The sight is worthy of the army of angels, worthy of patriarchs, prophets, the just—men in the very flower of youth, despising life, loving the Lord above parents, above children. Having the vitality of their age, they looked down on the temporary life in order to glorify God with their limbs. Becoming a spectacle for the world and for angels and human beings (1 Cor 4:9), they raised the fallen, they strengthened the ambivalent, they doubled the desire of the pious. All of them raised the one trophy on behalf of piety and were crowned with the one crown of justice too, in Christ Jesus our Lord, to whom be the glory and the power forever and ever. Amen.

5.4 Anon., *Life of Abraham of Qidun*[9]

21. When he arrived at the spot where the tavern was situated, he spent a little while looking around in case he should see her. Failing to find her, he spoke to the tavern keeper with a smile on his lips, "My friend, I've heard you have a pretty lass here; I'd like to see her." Seeing Abraham's venerable white hair, the tavern keeper thought ill of him inwardly, but nevertheless said in reply, "Yes, there is; she is indeed pretty." The blessed girl, you

---

9. Translated by Sebastian Brock and Susan Ashbrook Harvey, *Holy Women of the Syrian Orient* (Berkeley: University of California Press, 1987), 32–36. Reprinted by permission of the University of California Press.

should understand, was quite exceptionally beautiful. Her uncle then said to the tavern keeper, "What is her name? . . . so that we can enjoy ourselves together with her today. From what I've heard of her I am much attracted by her." The tavern keeper called to her and she came. When Abraham caught sight of her dolled up and dressed like a prostitute, his whole body nearly began to run with tears, but he valiantly gripped hold of his emotions lest she notice and run away. As they sat drinking, this amazing old man began to chat with her, and she drew close to him and started embracing him and kissing his neck. But as she caressed him, the smell of asceticism that issued from the blessed man's body hit her. Immediately she recalled the days of her own ascetic life, and choking with grief, she gasped, "Woe is me, me alone!" In astonishment the tavern keeper addressed her: "My lady Mary, you've been with us for two years to the day, and I've never heard you groan and say anything like that. What's the matter with you?" "Had I died three years ago, I would have received a great blessing," she replied. To prevent her realizing who he was, the blessed man said to her angrily, "Why do you have to recall your sins now that I've come?"

22. My beloved listeners, don't you suppose that she said in her heart, "How much the man resembles my uncle," or "Isn't his build like that of my father?" But God who alone is wise and loves mankind saw to it that she did not recognize him and so run away in panic. At that moment the blessed man brought out a daric and, handing it to the tavern keeper, said, "Take this, my friend, and prepare us a first class meal so that we can enjoy ourselves today with this lass. I've come a long way to see her." What wisdom of spirit, what true discernment in the company he kept! This man, who for fifty years had not even eaten any bread due to his ascetic way of life, now, for the sake of one soul, ate meat and drank wine, all in order to rescue a lost soul. The angel hosts stood in astonishment at the blessed man's discerning action, how with a good will and without any hesitation, he ate and drank, all in order to draw up a soul that had sunk into foul smelling mire. How great is the wisdom of the truly wise, what perception do those who truly understand possess! Come and stand in awe at the "folly" of a man perfected in wisdom!

Here is a man of sharp understanding who became a boorish fool in order to remove from the serpent's mouth the soul that had been swallowed up, who rescued and delivered from bonds and from the prison of darkness the soul that had been held captive, having strayed after vanity.

23. After they had chatted together, the girl said, "Please come into my bedroom so that we can sleep together." "Let's go in," he replied. On entering he espied a large bed made up, and of his own accord he sat down beside her. O perfect athlete of Christ, I know not what name I should give you, or what I should call you. Should I speak of you as a Nazirite, or someone who has compromised himself? Full of wisdom, or of folly? A man of discernment, or someone who has lost all sense of proportion? After fifty years of monastic life, sleeping on matting, how is it that you can sit down on such a bed? You did all this for the honor and glory of God: you made a long journey, you ate meat and drank wine, condescended to enter a tavern, all in order to save a lost soul. We hesitate to utter a single uplifting word to those present.

24. As he sat on the bed, the girl spoke to him: "Come, let me take off your shoes." "Shut the door first and then you can come and take them off." She objected and wanted to take off his shoes first, but he said no. So she shut the door and came back to him. "My lady Mary, draw close to me," he said. When she had done so, he grasped her firmly to prevent her escaping and, as though wanting to kiss her, he removed his helmet from his head and spoke to her with tears in his eyes: "My daughter Mary, don't you recognize me? Am I not your father Abraham? My beloved daughter, child of my dearest relations, don't you know who I am? Didn't I bring you up? What has happened to you, my daughter? Who has killed you this way—or so it seems? Where is that precious monastic habit you used to wear? Where is your ascetic way of life, where are the tears in your eyes? Where are your vigils, your bed on the ground? From what a height have you now sunk to such a pit as this! I brought you up as my daughter: why didn't you tell me when you committed the sin? I would have done penance for you along with my

beloved Ephrem. Why have you acted like this? What was the reason for your leaving me, throwing upon me an unutterable sadness? Who is without sin, apart from God alone?" As she listened to these words she became like a motionless stone in his hands, petrified with terror and fear. "Won't you speak to me, my daughter?" the blessed man went on, in tears. "Wasn't it for your sake that I have come here? The sin shall be upon me, and I will answer on your behalf to God on the day of judgment. I will be the one who does penance for this sin." He continued right up to midnight, begging her and admonishing her in tears. When she had plucked up enough courage, she said to him as she wept: "I cannot bring myself to look upon you, sir, seeing what a shameful thing I have done. How can I pray to God, now that I have befouled myself in this stench and mud?" The blessed man replied, "My daughter, I have taken upon myself your wrongdoing: God will require this sin at my hands. Just listen to me, and come back to our home. My beloved Ephrem is also full of grief because of you, and he makes supplication to God on your behalf: your soul is in his hands. Have pity on my old age, spare my white hairs, listen to your father's counsel, I beg of you." He said this, having fallen on his knees trying to persuade her; whereupon she replied, "If you are certain that I can repent, and that God will receive me, then I come and fall at your feet, supplicating your venerable person; I kiss your holy feet because your compassion stirred you to come after me in order to raise me up from this foul abyss of mine." Thus she spent the whole night in tears, saying, "How can I repay you, my father, for all that you have done for me?" When morning came, he said, "My daughter, let's get up and get away from here." "There's a little gold and a lot of clothes that I've picked up in the course of my life of shame, what should I do with them?" she asked. "Leave them all here; they belong to the Evil One," he said.

25. So they got up and left without further ado. He sat her down on the horse, while he walked ahead, leading it. He traveled happy at heart, like a shepherd once he had found his sheep that had gone astray, carrying it home in joy on his shoulders. Such was the blessed man's joy of mind as he traveled home.

When they arrived, he enclosed her in the inner part of the house where he had previously lived, while he took up residence in the outer part, which had formerly been her place. Dressed in sackcloth and humility, she spent her time in tears and vigil, fasting and showing great diligence in her penitence as, without any hesitation, she called upon God who has pity on sinners. Her repentance was completely sincere. This supplication and the reconciliation it effected astounded everyone. Who was so unfeeling that he did not open the eyes of his mind at her weeping? Who was so hard hearted that he failed to praise God when he heard the sound of her lamenting her sins? Compared with hers, our repentance is a mere shadow; compared with hers, our supplications are just dreamlike. Without any hesitation at all did she make supplication to God, asking him to forgive her what she had done. In order to provide a visible sign that God, the compassionate and the lover of mankind who receives the prayers of the penitent, accepted her back, a healing was effected through her prayer.

5.5 Nilus of Ancyra, *Letter 2.223* (*To Maximus the Presbyter*)[10]

If something has been recorded in the Old or New Testament to have happened historically, and this or that deed was manifestly accomplished, and we interpret it for our own purposes, using ideas and thoughts for our own spiritual edification, do not suppose that we have disregarded the letter, or rejected the history. By no means! We neither condemn nor reject the empirical event that has been committed to history. Since, however, we are "the world" (1 Cor 3:22), we benefit today by interpreting everything that happened yesterday for ourselves. For since today there is no Joseph, no Egypt, no King Hezekiah, no Judas the betrayer, no Lazarus dead and raised, no Simon Magus, etc., for this reason if [today] we see someone prudent, we call him "Joseph," an adulterous woman, we call her "Egyptian"; if a ruler is faithful to God and pious, he is named "Hezekiah." Everyone who betrays the Word of truth and casts others to death

---

10. Translated from the Greek text in J.-P. Migne, ed., *Patrologia Graeca*, vol. 79 (Paris: J.-P. Migne, 1865), cols. 316B–317A.

is acknowledged a "Judas." If the noblest man, having become negligent, sins, and afterwards repents and is made alive, clearly his mind died through error and was raised through repentance [= "Lazarus"]. But him who approaches the Church of God hypocritically and is baptized merely with water but not with the Holy Spirit we are wont to call a "Simon Magus." . . . So interpret for your own purposes all the things that happened figuratively (*typikōs*) to the ancients and were performed by them (cf. 1 Cor 10:11). For the Apostle says, "We are the temple of the living God" (2 Cor 6:16), not the one built by Solomon of stone (cf. 1 Kgs 6:1). "For everything is yours, whether the world, or the present, or the future" (1 Cor 3:22).

5.6 Gregory the Great, *Moralia on Job*[11]

5.6.1 Introductory Letter

3. But be it known that there are some parts [of the book of Job], which we go through in a historical exposition, some we trace out in allegory upon an investigation of the figurative meaning, some we open in the lessons of moral teaching alone, allegorically conveyed, while there are some few which, with more particular care, we search out in all these ways together, exploring them in a threefold method. For first, we lay the historical foundations; next, by pursuing the figurative sense, we erect a fabric of the mind to be a strong hold of faith; and moreover as the last step, by the grace of moral instruction, we, as it were, clothe the edifice with an overcast of coloring. . . .

5.6.2 *Moralia*, Book 4 (Excerpt from the "Moral" Interpretation of Job 3:3–4)

23. Blessed Job, observing how presumptuously humanity, after its soul fell from its original state, was lifted up in prosperity,

---

11. Translated by James Bliss and Charles Marriott, *Morals of the Book of Job by S. Gregory the Great*, Library of Fathers of the Holy Catholic Church (Oxford: James Henry Parker; J.G.F. and J. Rivington, 1844), 200–202. Revised and updated.

and with what dismay it was dashed by adverse fortune, falls back in imagination to that unalterable state which humanity might have kept in Paradise, and in what a miserable light we humans beheld the fallen condition of our mortal state of being, so marked with adversity and prosperity, he showed by cursing the same in these words:

Ver. 3. "Let the day perish wherein I was born; and the night wherein it was said, There is a male child conceived."

24. It seems as it were like day, when the good fortune of this world smiles upon us, but it is a day that ends in night, for temporal prosperity often leads to the darkness of affliction. This day of good fortune the Prophet had condemned, when he said, "Neither have I desired man's day, as you know" (Jer 17:16). And this night our Lord declared he was to suffer at the final close of his incarnation, when he declared by the Psalmist as if in the past, "My reins also instructed me in the night season" (Ps 16:7). But by "the day" may be understood the pleasures of sin, and by "the night" the inward blindness, whereby humanity suffers itself to be brought down to the ground in the commission of sin. And therefore humanity wishes the day may perish, that all the flattering arts which are seen in sin, by the strong hand of justice interposing, may be brought to nothing. It wishes also that the "night may perish," that what the blinded mind executes even in yielding consent, it may put away by the castigation of penance. . . .

25. "Let the day perish wherein I was born, and the night wherein it was said, There is a male child conceived": i.e., "Let the delight perish, which has hurried humanity into sin, and the unguarded frailness of our mind, whereby humanity was blinded even to the very darkness of consenting to evil." For while humanity does not heedfully mark the allurements of pleasure, it is even carried headlong into the night of the foulest practices. We must watch then with minds alive, that when sin begins to caress, the mind may perceive to what ruin it is being dragged. And hence the words are fitly added, "Let that day be darkness" (Job 3:4).

26. For "the day becomes darkness," when in the very commencement of the enjoyment, we see to what an end of ruin sin is hurrying us. We "turn the day into darkness," whenever by severely chastising ourselves, we turn to bitter the very sweets of evil enjoyment by the keen laments of penance, and, when we visit it with weeping, whenever we sin in gratification in our secret hearts. For because no believer is ignorant that the thoughts of the heart will be minutely examined at the Judgment—as Paul testifies, saying, "Their thoughts the meanwhile accusing or else excusing one another" (Rom 2:15)—Paul searches himself within, examining his own conscience without sparing before the Judgment, in order that the strict Judge may come now the more pleasingly disposed, in that he sees his guilt, which he is minded to examine, already chastised according to the sin. . . .

6.

Sacraments, Liturgy, and Moral Formation

INTRODUCTION

It is hard to overemphasize the role of sacramental and liturgical rituals in the moral as well as spiritual formation of Christians in the ancient church. Admonition to righteous living through preaching and instruction in the word of Scripture, beginning in the catechumenate but continuing well beyond baptism, was complemented by celebration or ritual enactment of the drama of sacred history, the denouement of which, it was believed, was playing out in the foreground of the church. Sacramental and liturgical rites were uniquely "mimetic." In one of the texts from the preceding chapter [5.1], Origen notes how both the Red Sea crossing and the crossing of the Jordan by the ancient people of God are mystically fulfilled "now" in the believer's passage through the waters of baptism (cf. 1 Cor 10:11). Sacramental and liturgical simulation of the ancient events is the outworking of a grace not restricted to their original occurrence. As Christian liturgy became increasingly more elaborate East and West, especially from the fourth century on, its power to reinforce religious allegiance and moral fidelity intensified.

Baptism was perhaps the rite most saturated with typological significance. Cyril of Jerusalem (ca. 315–ca. 386), in one of his so-called *Mystagogical Catecheses* [6.1], episcopal lectures given to the newly baptized, found no shortage of biblical types and images to depict the radical transformation that baptism evoked: shedding old clothes and donning new (baptizands were immersed in the nude and had a white robe placed on them afterward), and the death and burial simulated by immersion under water, were only two of these. Interestingly, Cyril acknowledges that baptism is a mimesis, a representation, but emphasizes that the salvation operative in it is altogether real. The baptismal liturgy was elaborate and intended to dramatize several sequences of regeneration. Theodore of Mopsuestia (ca. 350–ca. 428), in one of his *Catecheses* on baptism [6.2], describes some other details, including the formal renunciation of Satan (which culminated the exorcism that had begun in the catechumenate) and the "adhesion" (*syntaxis*) to Christ and the Trinity. These actions presupposed the doctrine of the "Two Ways" (Death and Life) that went all the way back to the *Didache* (see above, 3.1), since baptism was to be a moral and spiritual point of no return.

Ambrose of Milan, in an excerpt on the Eucharist from his treatise *On the Sacraments* [6.3], asserts a key principle of his liturgical theology as a whole, that it is Jesus Christ himself who operates through the sacraments, giving them transformative power. In the Eucharist it is his own proven Word, which was already active in the creation of the world, that remakes the simple elements of bread and wine into his body and blood, which in turn make new creatures (2 Cor 5:17) out of those who partake of them. I have chosen this text since it reflects a broader early Christian conviction that Christ's sacramental grace brings about the *ontological* change that underlies and enables moral change in believers.

With Augustine's *Sermon* 207 [6.4] we see clearly how the expanding celebrations and protocols of the liturgical year, in this case Lent, laid claim to the Christian's moral and spiritual progress. Augustine recommends prayer and fasting, and especially almsgiving or acts of mercy as well as proactive self-denial, as altogether appropriate penitential disciplines in the Lenten season preparing for the celebration of Christ's own passion.

The less-familiar Eastern Christian ascetical and mystical writer Pseudo-Dionysius the Areopagite (ca. 500), whose writings enjoyed significant legacies both East and West, demonstrates in his *Ecclesiastical Hierarchy* [6.5] the peculiar ascetical discipline built into the Divine Liturgy, on which this work is, in part, a commentary. When Dionysius speaks of "hierarchy," he means more than just the vertical arrangement of clerical and lay constituencies in the church; the term signals the whole schema of divine self-revelation, the gracious "ray" of divine light radiating through Scripture, through the very fabric of the intelligible and sensible universe, and through the structural and liturgical orders of the church. His supposition is that the church and its liturgical symbols are a kaleidoscopic image or imitation of the divine thearchy (Godhead), and in this passage he indicates how the hierarchs (bishops), priests, and deacons are charged (especially in their liturgical functions) to assimilate laypersons to the perfection to which they are called in their respective stations: first the novices being "purified" at their varied levels of maturity; then the intermediates, those progressing in the contemplation of divine things; and finally monks, the highest order of laity, who have achieved purification and are advancing toward the perfection of contemplation.

I conclude this chapter with an actual liturgical text—in this case a *kontakion*, or sermonic hymn (with choral refrains)—to show how moral mimesis worked within liturgy. Romanos the Melodist (ca. 490–ca. 556), a prolific hymnwriter of the early Byzantine period, crafted many of his *kontakia* to retell a biblical narrative in more amplified dramatic form (enhancing characterizations, introducing imaginary dialogues, highlighting ironies, etc.), but typically using short choral refrains between the stanzas in order for the audience to be drawn into the story and to respond to its impact. The particular sample here [6.6], from Romanos's *Kontakion on Judas*, exhibits this pattern. Judas's villainy is cast as a truly cosmic crime of betrayal of the Savior, in which all Christians are implicated by betraying him through their own sins, as the penitential refrain suggests: "Be merciful, merciful, merciful to us. You who are patient with all, and wait for all."

THE TEXTS

6.1 Cyril of Jerusalem, *Mystagogical Catechesis* 2 (on Baptism)[1]

2. Immediately when you entered [the baptismal font], you removed your garment, thus displaying an image of "putting off the old self with its deeds" (Col 3:9). Having stripped down, you were naked, and by this you imitated Christ stripped naked on the cross, by which nakedness he "divested himself of the principalities and powers" (Col 2:15), boldly triumphing over them on the tree. For because the enemy powers lurked in our [bodily] members, you may no longer wear that old garment—I do not mean at all the actual visible garment but rather your "old self, corrupt and deluded by its lusts" (Eph 4:22). May your soul, having once thrown off this old self, never put it on again, but say with the bride of Christ in the Song of Songs, "I have taken off my garment; how shall I put it on again?" (Song 5:3). How amazing! You were naked in the open view of everyone and not ashamed. In truth you bore the image of the protoplast Adam, who was naked in paradise and not ashamed (Gen 2:25).

3. Then after you were stripped naked, you were anointed from head to toe with exorcised oil, and you became partakers of the cultivated olive tree, Jesus Christ. For having been pruned from the wild olive tree, you were engrafted into the cultivated olive tree, and became partakers of the richness of the true olive tree (cf. Rom 11:17–24). Thus the exorcised oil constituted a symbol of communion in the richness of Christ, banishing the influence of every hostile influence arrayed against you. For just as the breathings of the holy upon you[2] and the invocation of the name of God, like a robust flame, burned away and banished demons, so too this exorcised oil, through the invocation of God and prayer, acquires power sufficient not only to burn and cleanse the traces of sins but also to banish the invisible powers of the Evil One.

---

1. Translated from the Greek text in J.-P. Migne, ed., *Patrologia Graeca*, vol. 33 (Paris: J.-P. Migne, 1857), cols. 1077A–1081B.
2. The ancient catechumenate included the bishop ritually "breathing" on catechumens to exorcise demons in preparation for their baptism.

4. Thereupon you were escorted to the baptismal pool, just as Christ was carried from the cross to the tomb that you see before you. And each of you was asked whether you believed in the name of the Father, Son, and Holy Spirit. You recited the saving confession, and you descended into the water and ascended from it three times, thereby symbolically indicating the three-day burial of Christ in the tomb. For inasmuch as our Savior spent three days and three nights in the heart of the earth, you too, by your first ascent [from the water] imitated Christ's first day in the earth, and by your descent his first night. For just as one no longer sees at night, and yet sees in the light of day, so too in your baptismal descent you saw nothing, as in the night, but when you ascended you were as in the light of day. At one and the same time you died and were born, and the saving water was simultaneously your grave and your mother. What Solomon said for others may very well apply to you here, when he speaks of "a time to be born, and a time to die" (Eccl 3:2). But for you the converse is the case: "a time to die, and a time to be born." Both happened at the same time. Your death and your birth were concurrent.

5. How extraordinary and paradoxical! We did not actually die; nor were we buried or crucified or raised. Rather, this was all an imitation, as in an image; but our salvation was real. Christ himself was actually crucified, actually buried, and truly raised; and he has graced us with all these things, in order that, by participating in his sufferings through imitation, we might really and truly attain salvation. What surpassing loving-kindness! Christ received the nails in his undefiled hands and feet, and felt bitter pain, while I, without pain or toil, was granted salvation through fellowship in his sufferings (cf. Phil 3:10).

6.2 Theodore of Mopsuestia, *Catechesis on Baptism*[3]

When you go to be enrolled in the hope of acquiring the abode and citizenship of heaven, you have, in the ceremony of exorcism, a kind of law-suit with the Demon, and by a divine verdict you receive your freedom from his servitude. And thus you recite the words of the profession of faith and of prayer, and through them you make an engagement and a promise to God, before the priests, that you will remain in the love of the divine nature—concerning which, if you think the right things, it will be to you the source of great benefits; and it consists of the Father, the Son and the Holy Spirit—and that you will live in this world to the best of your ability in a way that is consonant with the life and citizenship of heaven. It is right now that you should receive the teaching of the ceremonies that take place in the Sacrament itself, because if you learn the reason for each one of them, you will acquire a knowledge that is by no means small. After you have been taken away from the servitude of the Tyrant by means of the words of exorcism, and have made solemn engagements to God along with the recitation of the Creed, you draw near to the Sacrament itself; you must learn how this is done.

You stand barefooted on sackcloth while your outer garment is taken off from you, and your hands are stretched towards God in the posture of one who prays. In all this you are in the likeness of the posture that fits the words of exorcism, as in it you have shown your old captivity and the servitude which through a dire punishment you have rendered to the Tyrant; but it is right that after you have cast away that posture and those memories you should draw near to the Sacrament which implies participation in the future benefits. You recall in your memory your old tribulations in order that you may all the better know the nature of the things which you cast away and that of the things to which you will be transferred.

First you genuflect while the rest of your body is erect, and

---

3. Translated from the Syriac version by Alphonse Mingana, *Commentary of Theodore of Mopsuestia on the Lord's Prayer and on the Sacraments of Baptism and the Eucharist*, Woodrooke Studies 6 (Cambridge: Heffer, 1933), 35–38, 43–45. Slightly revised.

in the posture of one who prays you stretch your arms towards God. As we have all of us fallen into sin and been driven to the dust by the sentence of death, it is right for us to "bow our knees in the name of Jesus Christ," as the blessed Paul said, and to "confess that Jesus Christ is Lord, to the glory of God his Father" (Phil 2:11). In this confession we show the things that accrued to us from the divine nature through the economy of Christ our Lord, whom (God) raised up to heaven and showed as Lord of all and head of our salvation. Because all these things have to be performed by us all, who "are fallen to the earth" according to the words of the blessed Paul, it is with justice that you, who through the Sacrament become partakers of the ineffable benefits, to which you have been called by your faith in Christ, bow your knees, and make manifest your ancient fall, and worship God, the cause of those benefits.

The rest of all your body is erect and looks towards heaven. In this posture you offer prayer to God, and implore him to grant you deliverance from the ancient fall and participation in the heavenly benefits. While you are in this posture, the persons who are appointed for the service draw near to you and say to you something more than that which the angel who appeared to the blessed Cornelius said to him: your prayers have been heard and your supplications answered. God has looked upon your tribulations which you were previously undergoing, and had mercy upon you because you were for a long time captives of the Tyrant, and served a cruel servitude to him. He saw the number and the nature of the calamities which you have endured, and this moved him to deliver you from that servitude and from the great number of your ancient tribulations, and to bring you to freedom and grant you to participate in the ineffable heavenly benefits, which immediately after you have received, you become undoubtedly free from all calamities. It is now time for you to learn the things through which you will surely receive deliverance from your ancient tribulations, and enjoy the good things that have been shown to you.

What are then the engagements and promises which you make at that time, and through which you receive deliverance from the ancient tribulations, and participation in the future benefits?

> I abjure Satan and all his angels, and all his service, and all his deception, and all his worldly glamour; and I engage myself, and believe, and am baptized in the name of the Father, and of the Son, and of the Holy Spirit.

The deacons who at that time draw near to you prepare you to recite these words. It is in place here to explain to you the power of these words, in order that you may know the force of the engagements, promises and words of asseveration through which you receive the happiness of this great gift. Because the Devil, to whom you had listened, was for you the cause of numerous and great calamities—as he has begun (his work) from the time of the fathers of your race—you promise to abjure him, since facts themselves and your own experience had made you feel his injuries. This is the reason why you say "I abjure Satan." Formerly, even if you wished it, you did not dare to make use of these words, because you were afraid of his servitude, but as you have, by a divine decree, received deliverance from him, you proclaim and abjure him with confidence and by your own words, and this is the reason why you say "I abjure Satan." In this you imply both your present separation from him and the former association that you had with him. Indeed, no one says that he abjures a thing with which he had formerly no association. The use of this expression is especially incumbent upon you as you had relation with him from the time of your forefathers, together with that cruel and ancient pact, which resulted in the calamitous servitude to him, under which you lived....

After having said: "I abjure Satan, and his angels, and his service, and his deception, and all his worldly glamour" you add:

> And I engage myself, and believe and am baptized in the name of the Father, and of the Son and of the Holy Spirit.

As when you say "I abjure (Satan)" you mean to reject him for always, and not to revert to him nor be pleased to associate yourself with him anymore, so also when you say "I engage myself before God" you show that you will remain steadfastly with him, that you will henceforth be unshakably with him, that you will never separate yourself from him, and that you will think it higher than anything else to be and to live with him and to conduct yourself in a way that is in harmony with his commandments.

The addition "And I believe" is necessary because the person who draws near to God ought to believe that God is, as the blessed Paul said. As divine nature is invisible, faith is called to the help of the person who draws near to it, and who promises to be constantly in its household. The good things that (God) prepared for us, through the economy of Christ our Lord, are likewise invisible and unspeakable, and since it is in their hope that we draw near to him and receive the sacrament of baptism, faith is required so that we may possess a strong belief without doubt concerning these good things which are prepared for us and which are now invisible.

You add also the sentence "and I am baptized" to that of "and I believe" so that you may draw near to the gift of the holy baptism, in the hope of future benefits, and be thus enabled to be reborn and to die with Christ and rise with him from there, and so that after having received another birth, instead of your first one, you may be able to participate in heaven. As long as you are mortal by nature you are not able to enter the abode of heaven, but after you have cast away such a nature in baptism and have risen also with Christ through baptism, and received the symbol of the new birth which we are expecting, you will be seen as a citizen of heaven and an heir of the Kingdom of Heaven.

To all the above (sentences) you add:

> In the name of the Father, and of the Son, and of the Holy Spirit.

This is the divine nature, this is the eternal Godhead, this is the cause of everything, and this is that which first created us and now is renewing us. This is, indeed, the Father, the Son and the Holy Spirit. It is to it that we are drawing near now, and it is to it that we are rightly making our promises, because it has been to us the cause of numerous and great benefits, as at the beginning even so now. It is to it that we make these ineffable promises, and it is in it that we engage ourselves to believe henceforth. It is in its names that we are baptized, and through it that we expect to receive the future good things which are now promised to us as in a symbol, and it is to it that we look for the happiness which is to come, when we shall rise in reality from the dead, and become immortal and immutable in our nature, and heirs and partakers of the abode and citizenship of heaven.

These engagements and promises you make in the posture which we have described above, while your knee is bowed to the ground both as a sign of adoration which is due from you to God, and as a manifestation of your ancient fall to the ground; the rest of your body is erect and looks upwards towards heaven, and your hands are outstretched in the guise of one who prays so that you may be seen to worship the God who is in heaven, from whom you expect to rise from your ancient fall. This is the reason why you have, through the promises and engagements which we have already described, directed your course towards him and have promised to him that you will make yourself worthy of the expected gift. After you have looked towards him with outstretched hands, asked grace from him, risen from your fall and rejoiced in (future) benefits, you will necessarily receive the first-fruits of the sacrament which we believe to be the earnest of the good and ineffable things found in heaven. When you have, therefore, made your promises and engagements, the priest draws near to you, wearing, not his ordinary garments or the covering with which he was covered before, but clad in a robe of clean and radiant linen, the joyful appearance of which denotes the joy of the world to which you will move in the future, and the shining color of which designates your own radiance in the life to come, while its cleanness indicates the ease and happiness of the next world. . . .

6.3 Ambrose of Milan, *On the Sacraments*, Book 4 (on the Eucharist)[4]

4.13. Who, then, is the author of the sacraments but the Lord Jesus? From heaven those sacraments came; for all counsel is from heaven. But it was truly a great and divine miracle that

---

4. Translated by T. Thompson, *St. Ambrose: On the Mysteries and the Treatise on the Sacraments*, Translations of Christian Literature, Series 3: Liturgical Texts (London and New York: SPCK, 1919), 109–13. Revised and updated.

God rained down manna from heaven, and the people ate without toiling (Exod 16:4–36; Ps 78:23–25; cf. John 6:31–35).

4.14. You say perhaps, "My bread is of the usual kind." But that bread is bread before the words of the sacraments; when consecration has been added, from bread it becomes the flesh of Christ. Let us therefore prove this. How can that which is bread be the body of Christ? By consecration. But in what words and in whose language is the consecration? Those of the Lord Jesus. For all the other things which are said in the earlier parts of the service are said by the priest—praises are offered to God, prayer is asked for the people, for kings, and the rest; when it comes to the consecration of the venerable sacrament, the priest no longer uses his own language, but he uses the language of Christ. Therefore, the word of Christ consecrates this sacrament.

4.15. What is the word of Christ? That, to be sure, whereby all things are made. The Lord commanded, and the heaven was made; the Lord commanded, and the earth was made; the Lord commanded, and the seas were made; the Lord commanded, and every creature was produced (Gen 1:1–2:1). You see, therefore, how effective the word of Christ is. If, therefore, there is such power in the word of the Lord Jesus, that the things which were not began to be, how much more is it effective, that things previously existing should, without ceasing to exist, be changed into something else? The heaven was not, the sea was not, the earth was not; but hear David saying, "He spoke, and they were made: he commanded, and they were created" (Ps 33:9).

4.16. Therefore, that I may answer you, the bread was not the body of Christ before consecration; but after consecration, I tell you, it is now the body of Christ. "He spoke, and it was made: he commanded, and it was created." You yourself formerly existed, but you were an old creature; after you were consecrated, you began to be a new creature. Will you know how you are a new creature? Everyone, it says, in Christ is a new creature (2 Cor 5:17).

4.17. Hear, then, how the word of Christ is wont to change every creature, and changes, at will, the ordinances of nature. You ask: In what way? Just listen. First of all, let us take an example from human generation. It is usual that a human being is not born save from a man and a woman and the use of marriage; because the Lord willed it, because he chose this mystery,[5] Christ was born of the Holy Spirit and the Virgin, that is, the mediator between God and humanity, the man Christ Jesus. You see, then, that he was born contrary to the ordinances and course of nature, he was born as man from a virgin.

4.18. Hear another example. The people of the Jews were hard pressed by the Egyptians; they were shut in by the sea. At the divine command Moses touched the waters with his rod, and the wave divided, certainly not according to the use of its own nature, but according to the grace of the heavenly command (Exod 14:21–22). Hear still another. The people thirsted, they came to the spring. The spring was bitter; holy Moses cast wood into the spring, and the spring which had been bitter was made sweet (Exod 15:23–25), that is, it changed the use of its nature, it received the sweetness of grace. Hear also a fourth example. The axe head had fallen into the waters; as iron it sank by its own use. Elisha cast wood; straightway the iron rose, and swam upon the waters (2 Kgs 6:5–6), certainly contrary to the use of iron, for the matter of iron is heavier than the element of water.

4.19. From all these examples, then, do you not understand how effectual is the heavenly word? If the heavenly word was effectual in the earthly spring, if it was effectual in other things, is it not effectual in the heavenly sacraments? Therefore you have learned that what was bread becomes the body of Christ, and that wine and water are put into the chalice, but become blood by the consecration of the heavenly word.

4.20. But perhaps you say, "I do not see the appearance of blood." But it has the likeness; for just as you have taken the likeness of the death (Rom 6:5), so also you drink the likeness of the precious blood, that there may be no shrinking from actual

---

5. I.e., the mystery of his own incarnation.

blood, and yet the price of redemption may affect its work. You have learned, therefore, that what you receive is the body of Christ.

6.4 Augustine, *Sermon* 207 (*On the Beginning of Lent*)[6]

1. With the help of the mercy of the Lord our God, the temptations of this age, the crafty traps of the devil, the toils of this world, the allurements of the flesh, the swirl of turbulent times, and all bodily and spiritual adversity, are to be overcome by almsgiving and fasting and prayer. Christians ought to be fervently engaged in these things throughout their lives; much more so then at the approach of the great festival of Easter, which rouses our minds as it comes round again each year, renewing in them the salutary memory of what mercy our Lord, the only Son of God, has bestowed on us, of how he fasted and prayed for us.

"Alms," of course, comes from a Greek word meaning "mercy." What greater mercy, though, could there be toward the miserable, than that which pulled the Creator down from heaven, and clothed the Founder of the earth in an earthly body; which made the one who abides equal in eternity to the Father, equal to us in mortality, imposing the form of a servant (cf. Phil 2:7) on the Lord of the world; so that Bread itself would be hungry (John 6:35; Luke 4:2), Fullness be thirsty (cf. John 4:7; 19:28; Col 2:9), Strength become weak (cf. 2 Cor 12:9; 11:29; Luke 22:41–44), Health would be wounded, Life would die (cf. John 14:6). And all this to feed our hunger, water our drought, comfort our infirmity, extinguish our iniquity, kindle our charity. What greater mercy, than for the Creator to be created, the Master to serve (cf. John 13:13-14), the Redeemer to be sold (cf. Matt 26:14–15; 27:9), the One who exalts to be humbled (cf. Luke 18:14), the One who raises up (cf. John 6:54) to be slain? We, in the matter of giving alms, are instructed to give bread to the hungry (cf. Isa 58:7); he, in order to give himself to us

---

6. Translated by Edmund Hill, *Works of St. Augustine* 3/6 (New Rochelle, NY: New City Press, 1993), 109–10. Slightly modified. Reprinted by permission of New City Press.

in our hunger, first surrendered himself for us to his enemies' anger. We are instructed to welcome the stranger; he, for our sakes, came down to his own place, and his own people did not welcome him (cf. John 1:11).

Let our soul, in a word, "bless him who shows himself gracious to all its iniquities, who heals all its infirmities, who redeems its life from corruption, who crowns it with compassion and mercy, who satisfies its desire with good things" (Ps 103:2–5). And so let us perform our alms and deeds of kindness all the more lavishly, all the more frequently, the nearer the day approaches on which is celebrated the alms, the kindness that has been done to us. Because fasting without kindness and mercy is worth nothing to the one who's fasting.

2. Let us also fast by humbling our souls, as the day approaches on which the Master humbled himself, "becoming obedient even to the death of the cross" (Phil 2:8). Let us imitate his cross, pacifying and nailing our lusts with the nails of abstinence. Let us chastise our bodies, and subject them to hard service; and to avoid slipping into unlawful pleasures because of the unruliness of the flesh, in breaking it in let us deprive it to some extent even of lawful ones. . . .

6.5 Pseudo-Dionysius the Areopagite, *Ecclesiastical Hierarchy*[7]

5.1.7. So it has been shown how the order of hierarchs[8] generates complete sanctification and perfection, how the order of the priests generates light and illumination, and how the order of the deacons[9] serves purification and discerns [who are the imperfect needing perfection]. Clearly the order of hierarchs is not restricted solely to the ministry of perfection; it too knows how to illuminate and purify, and subsumes in itself the priests' own

---

7. Translated from the Greek text edited by Günter Heil and Adolf Ritter, *Corpus Dionysiacum* II, Patristische Texte und Studien, vol. 36 (Berlin: Walter de Gruyter, 1991), 109–10, 115–16.

8. "Hierarchs" for Dionysius designates the order of bishops (patriarchs, metropolitans, and local bishops).

9. Dionysius calls the deacons *leituourgoi*, accentuating their assisting role in liturgy and in worshipers' moral and spiritual formation.

illuminative and cathartic knowledge. For while the lower powers cannot transgress the dignities of their superiors, as it would be sacrilegious for them to undertake such arrogance, the more divine powers enjoy, along with their own knowledge, the sacred knowledge of those powers subordinate to their perfection. Since, nevertheless, the sacerdotal ranks are images of the harmonious and unconfused order of divine activities, and therein demonstrate their properly appointed illuminations, these ranks have been arranged in first, middle, and last sacred activities and orders by hierarchical distinction, thus manifesting, as I said, the orderliness and unconfused nature of the divine operations. The Thearchy [Godhead] first purifies minds that it indwells, then it illuminates them, and, once illuminated, it consecrates them for deiform perfection. So naturally the hierarchy, as an image of the divine, divides itself into distinct orders and powers, clearly revealing the divine activities in their all-holy and pure ranks, which remain steadfast, unconfused, and secure.

6.1.1-3. I must now explain in sequence the three ranks of initiates[10] who are subordinate to the sacerdotal orders.

Let us say that the ranks of those being purified consist of those multitudes who are kept separate from holy activities and the performance of sacred [sacramental and liturgical] rites, as I have already noted. The first such rank of initiates includes those still assigned to the deacons to be formed and shaped by the life-bearing oracles [of Holy Scripture] to produce new life. Some are those still being recalled, through instruction in Scripture's beneficial oracles, to the holy life from which they fell away. Others are those who, still cowering in the face of contrary fears, are being encouraged under the influence of Scripture's empowering oracles. Others, moreover, are those still in the process of transitioning from wretched to holy endeavors. Finally, there are those in this first rank being led toward, but not yet having achieved holy constancy in more godlike and resolute habitudes. Altogether, these groups constitute the rank of those being purified under the life-bearing and purifying power of the deacons. The deacons, with their sacred aptitudes, work to consecrate

---

10. Lit. "those being perfected," i.e., the ranks of laypersons.

them such that, being fully purified, they are translated to illuminative contemplation of, and communion in, the most dazzling sacramental rites.

The intermediate rank of initiates includes those who are contemplating certain sacred things, and who participate in complete purity proportionate to their ability. They are assigned to the priests for their illumination. To me it seems obvious that, having been cleansed of every unholy taint, and having attained the pure and immovable stability of their own minds, they are led through sacred activity to the consistent habit and capacity of contemplation and commune accordingly in the sublimely divine symbols. In their contemplations and their communion they are filled with every holy joy, and they rise up to the divine passion for their acquired knowledge in proportion to their anagogical abilities.[11] This, I suggest, is the order of holy people, such as has passed through total purification and, so far as religiously legitimate, become worthy of holy visions of and communing in the most illustrious sacred rites.

Of all the initiates, however, the most exalted rank is the holy order of monks, who have undergone absolute purification owing to the complete and total purity of their proper activities. To the permissible extent, they have arrived at noetic contemplation of the sacred [sacramental and liturgical] activities, and been entrusted with the hierarchs' perfecting powers, and been instructed in their inspired illuminative and hierarchic traditions. So in their own knowledge of holy things they are uplifted, proportionate to their ability, to the most complete perfection. Hence our reverend leaders have deemed them worthy of holy appellations, some calling them "therapeutae" [healers] and others "monks" owing to their impeccable service and devoted care toward God, as well as their undivided and unified way of life which, as it were, singularly focuses them on the holy ingathering of divided things, as they aspire to the deiform Unity and perfection in the love of God. . . .

---

11. "Anagogical," for Dionysius, indicates the "uplifting" of lowly created beings to superior divine realities as a grace intrinsic to God's self-revelation in Scripture and in the church's sacramental and liturgical mysteries.

6.6 Romanos the Melodist, *Kontakion on Judas* (Stanzas 1–3, 22–23)[12]

1. Who, upon hearing it, was not horrified? Who, when seeing it, did not tremble? Jesus kissed by deceit! Christ betrayed by envy, God snatched by design! What kind of earth countenanced this appalling act? What kind of sea submitted to watching this wicked deed? How did heaven abide, how did the air endure, how did the world go on existing when the Judge was being sold and handed over?

Refrain: *Merciful, merciful, be merciful to us, You who endure all and wait upon all*

2. When he meditated his treachery, when he planned your murder—this very one whom you had shown affection and yet rejected you, this one whom you had called and yet forsook you, this one whom you honored and yet mocked you—you thereupon, being compassionate and long-suffering, looked to show the killer your unspeakable loving-kindness. You filled up the basin, bowed your head, and became servant of servants, and Judas presented you his feet for you to wash them, O Redeemer!

Refrain: *Merciful, merciful, be merciful to us, You who endure all and wait upon all*

3. With water you washed the feet of the very one who ran to betray you, and you fed with mystical food the very nemesis of your tender mercy, who was stripped naked of your blessing. You exalted the beggar with graces, you lavished the pitiable rogue with gifts, making him wealthy and blessed. At his bidding he had command of demons, deliverance from toils, and instead of all these he was torn apart, and the murderer had no compunction.

---

12. Translated from the Greek text edited by Paul Maas and C. A. Trypanis, *Sancti Romani Melodi Cantica: Cantica Genuina* (Oxford: Oxford University Press, 1963), 123–24, 130–31.

Refrain: *Merciful, merciful, be merciful to us, You who endure all and wait upon all*

22. Stay a little while, you total wretch, in order to see irreversible judgment. Your own conscience condemns you, such that you will know what you have done while you die a frightening death. For you a tree becomes like an executioner, Rendering you the pay that you deserve. Where is your money now, lover of riches? But you will give that away also, and yet not save yourself with your ill-timed repentance, because you betrayed the true wealth of the soul: Christ!

Refrain: *Merciful, merciful, be merciful to us, You who endure all and wait upon all*

23. Holy, holy, holy, Thrice-Holy is the God of all, rescue your servants from the Fall, and raise your creature to flee from such a peril. So then recognizing all this, brothers and sisters, and observing the fall of the seller, let us plant our feet firmly; let us take our steps in upward ascents through the Creator's commandments, and flee the road to Hell, crying out to our Redeemer,

Refrain: *Merciful, merciful, be merciful to us, You who endure all and wait upon all.*

7.

Habituating Virtues and Eradicating Vices

INTRODUCTION

In my general introduction to this volume, I already spelled out the importance in early Christian ethics of the notions of virtue and vice. Moral excellence depended foremost not on intermittently submitting to commandments or directives but on sustained consistency both in moral vision (projecting salutary ends for one's actions) and in concrete actions themselves. The key link here was virtue, which Aristotle defined in terms of *hexeis*, variously translated "habits," "dispositions," "conditions," or "capacities" of the soul. We attain virtue, he said, as a result of performing just and temperate acts, and yet virtue must become the basis for continuing to perform them.[1] Virtues are habituated dispositions and also character traits of the virtuous person. What is more, healthy emotions accompany the virtues, and as I mentioned earlier, the virtues in Christian usage often sound precisely like healthy emotional states (humility, patience, endurance, kindness, etc.), just as the vices sound like sinful or detrimental emotional states. Though Aristotle had claimed that one was morally accountable for the virtues and vices themselves, not for their attendant emotions, Christian writers in many cases followed Stoic teaching that one was

---

1. See Aristotle's *Nicomachean Ethics* 1105B.

137

indeed accountable for appropriate moral "use" of the emotions. After all, were not many emotions intrinsically tied up with dispositions to virtue and vice?

The apologist and moralist Lactantius, at the beginning of the Constantinian age, largely presupposes this view of virtue and vice in the selection from his *Divine Institutes* [7.1], a large work that depicts Christianity as inaugurating a veritable moral and religious revolution, and heightening once for all the battle between good and evil. For the Christian living in a society that is still saturated with paganism, virtue must endure dispositionally, otherwise the ever-resilient vices immediately fill the vacuum and stifle all moral progress. In another passage not included here, Lactantius explains that God allows moral evil to subsist precisely because resistance to it is what strengthens virtue.[2]

Later in the fourth century, Gregory of Nyssa, in his treatise on *The Creation of Humanity*, one of the most important works of theological anthropology from Christian antiquity, contemplated at length how the human creature, created in an original state of perfection in the image of God (Gen 1:26–27), could in turn "invent" moral evil and the vices that actualize it. It was a vexing question. Even if this could be attributed to God's provision for human freedom, would there not have to be an antecedent flaw in the creature in order for him or her to misuse that freedom in the first place? And would not such a flaw reflect back on the Creator? I cannot outline Gregory's complex answer in detail, but the gist of it is that in foreseeing the Adamic fall, the Creator already outfitted human beings with certain elements of the animal or "irrational" creation, which were in turn capable of being oriented either to good or bad purposes. The selected text here [7.2] assumes that a result of the fall is a perversion of one of those irrational elements, the liability to "passions" (*pathē*), not in this instance healthy emotions but "vices," especially those related to unbridled desire or anger. Even survival instincts can take on a vicious life of their own. No matter the status of the divine image (*eikōn*), human beings are quite capable of undergoing ever greater assimilation (*homoiōsis*) to

---

2. Lactantius, *Divine Institutes* 5.7.

the beasts, betraying their true vocation of assimilation to God through the virtues. And yet Gregory recognizes that the "passible" faculties that give rise to emotions are intrinsically good because created by God. These faculties can be given to sound "use" (*chrēsis*), and with the intervention of reason otherwise unhealthy emotions can be transmuted to virtuous ones that advance one's moral progress. This principle will become crucial with monastic writers, including Evagrius, Diadochus [7.5], and Maximus [8.6.1].

Evagrius, in the passage from his treatise *To Eulogius* [7.3], propounds a major principle of the early monastic wisdom tradition: that virtue is excellent in its own right, and that it seeks no honor or repute from the outside because it is inherently, indeed supremely, honorable. Pursuing accolades for one's ascetical achievements defeats their very purpose. Vigilantly maintaining an attitude of repentance and compunction goes far to quell the temptation to pride. In other works Evagrius also detailed and discussed the "eight deadly vices." He calls them "thoughts" (*logismoi*), which spring up in the soul because of demonic infestation and manifest as destructive passions.[3] John Cassian appropriated much of Evagrius's thinking on the deadly vices, transmitting it into Western monasticism, and the passage here [7.4] from Cassian's *Conferences* takes up the causal links among the passions and the need to thwart the chain reaction by which they erupt. For many of the monastic writers of antiquity, dealing with the passions, or vices, is akin to a labor of constantly and vigilantly putting out fires in the soul, and mastering the interrelation between the vices is a vital ascetical discipline in its own right.

Evagrian influence clearly shows up as well in the monastic writer Diadochus of Photiki (ca. 400–ca. 486) in northern Greece, in whose works many significant themes of Eastern monastic spiritual doctrine intersect. The passages here from Diadochus's *Chapters on Spiritual Knowledge* [7.5] address two such themes. One recalls how virtue entails the appropriate use of the emotions, in this case anger deployed in the mode of

---

3. See especially Evagrius's treatises *On Thoughts* and *On the Eight Thoughts*.

righteous indignation against sin.[4] The other broaches the capital theme of *apatheia*, one of the most misunderstood concepts of monastic moral teaching by modern critics. "Impassibility" is probably not the most auspicious translation of *apatheia* in Greek, since it might imply an utterly "passionless" state of being. In writers like Diadochus, Mark the Monk, or Evagrius, it indicates a state of ultimate stability, serenity, or imperturbability of the soul's passible functions—*not* their annihilation. Since certain emotional states are indispensable to the moral health of the soul, sheer passionlessness is out of the question.

The last text of this chapter showcases a very different genre of moral instruction on the virtues and vices in early Christian literature. It is a segment from the *Psychomachia* (*Battle of the Soul*) of the Latin Christian poet Prudentius (348–ca. 410) in Spain. This poem is an extended allegory of the strife within the soul between virtues and vices, personified as female characters (since abstract ideas were feminine nouns in Latin) struggling to gain control and to win the moral day. It is a bloodbath, a fight to the death, with rule of the soul as the crown of victory. This particular sequence [7.6] has the seductress Indulgence (*Luxuria*) pitted against Soberness (*Sobrietas*). With its lively and picturesque drama, the *Psychomachia* had a substantial afterlife in medieval Christianity in the West.

THE TEXTS

7.1 Lactantius, *Divine Institutes*, Book 7[5]

10. Let us turn now to those things which oppose virtue, such as we can also muster in evidence of the immortality of the soul. All vices are temporary, for they are incited for the present moment. The violent impulse of anger subsides once revenge is taken. Lust ends with the arrival of bodily pleasure. Greed

---

4. For this same motif in Evagrius, see his *On Thoughts* 5.16–17.
5. Translated from the Latin text edited by Eberhard Heck and Antonie Wlosok, *L. Caelius Firmianus Lactantius Divinarum Institutionum libri septem*, fasc. 4, Bibliotheca Scriptorum Graecorum et Romanorum Teubneriana (Berlin: Walter de Gruyter, 2011), 680–81.

ends either when it satisfactorily gets what it covets or when agitations from other emotions cancel it out. Ambition wanes when the honors it craves are obtained. Similarly, other vices cannot hold their ground and endure, but are ended by the very enjoyment they desire. Thus they come and go. Virtue, however, remains perpetual without interruption, and cannot be separated from someone once he or she has grasped it. For if it has an interval, or if we are able to be without it for a time, then the vices that constantly assail virtue will resume immediately. If virtue deserts, or at some point withdraws, then it was not grasped in the first place; but when it truly establishes a secure home for itself, it necessarily abides in our every action, and cannot dispel and banish vice unless it fortifies the heart it occupies with a perpetual guard. The perpetuity of virtue therefore signals that the human soul, if it has taken on virtue, is itself permanent, since virtue is perpetual and only the human soul acquires it.

Because the vices oppose virtue, their entire scheme is also opposed to it. For the vices are disruptions or perturbations of the soul, while virtue, conversely, soothes and calms the soul. And since the vices are temporary and short-lived, virtue is perpetual, constant, and always consistent with itself. Since the product of the vices is pleasures, those pleasures are equally temporary and short-lived, the product and reward of virtue is everlasting. Whereas the profit of vice is immediate, the advantage of virtue lies in the future. So it is the case that there is no reward for virtue in this [temporary] life, since virtue itself continues in existence. For as vices are completed with their own activation, and their pleasures and rewards follow, so then virtue, when it is completed, has its own subsequent reward. Virtue, however, is not completed except in death, so its reward comes posthumously. In his *Tusculan Disputations*, Cicero sensed, however dubiously, that the supreme good of humanity is not realized until after death: "A man shall go to his death, if events allow, with a confident spirit, as in death we know that there is either the supreme good or else no evil."[6] Death therefore does not extinguish a man, but sends him to the reward of his virtue.

6. Cicero, *Tusculan Disputations* 1.46.110; cf. also Cicero, *Republic* 6.26.29.

As Cicero also adduces, however, anyone who has polluted himself or herself with vice and wicked deeds, and become enslaved to pleasure,[7] is damned and will suffer eternal punishment. This is what Holy Scripture calls the "second death" (Rev 2:11; 20:6, 14; 21:8), which is perpetual and full of excruciating pain. For just as two lives are proposed for humanity, one for the soul and the other for the body, so too humanity has two deaths, one for the body, which all of us must undergo according to nature, and the other for the soul, a death that wickedness can incur and virtue avoid. And just as this life is temporary and bound by limits because it is bodily, death is equally time-bound and has its determined end since it too is bodily.

7.2 Gregory of Nyssa, *On the Creation of Humanity*[8]

18. I think that from the beginning all our passions issue as from a spring, and pour their flood over human life. An evidence of my words is the kinship of passions which appears in ourselves and in irrational animals. For it is not allowable to ascribe the first beginnings of our constitutional liability to passion to that human nature which was fashioned in the divine likeness (Gen 1:26–27); but as irrational life first entered into the world, and humanity, for reasons already mentioned, took something of its nature (specifically I mean the mode of procreation), humanity accordingly took at the same time a share of the other attributes beheld in that irrational nature. For the likeness of humanity to God is not found in anger, nor is pleasure a mark of the superior [rational] nature; cowardice also, and boldness, and the desire of gain, and the dislike of loss, and all the like, are far removed from that stamp which indicates divinity.

These attributes, then, human nature took to itself from the side of irrational creatures; for those qualities with which irrational animals were armed for self-preservation, when transferred to human life, became passions. For the carnivorous ani-

---

7. Cicero, *Tusculan Disputations* 1.30.72.

8. Translated by William Moore and Henry Austin Wilson, *Gregory of Nyssa: Dogmatic Treatises*, Nicene and Post-Nicene Fathers, 2nd series, vol. 5 (Edinburgh: T&T Clark, 1893), 407–9. Revised and updated.

mals are preserved by their anger, and those which breed are preserved largely by their love of pleasure; cowardice preserves the weak, fear that which is easily taken by more powerful animals, and greediness those of great bulk; and to miss anything that tends to pleasure is for irrational creatures a matter of pain. All these and the like affections entered the human composition by reason of the animal mode of procreation.

Grant me to describe the human image by comparison with a wonderful piece of modeling. For, as one may see among models those carved shapes which the artisans of such things craft for the wonder of their audiences, tracing out upon a single head two forms of faces, so also a human being seems to me to bear a double likeness to opposite things—being fashioned in the deiform element of the mind to divine beauty, but bearing, in the passionate impulses that arise in a human, a likeness to the irrational nature. Often even human reason is rendered irrational, and obscures the better element by the worse through its inclination and disposition towards what is irrational; for whenever a human being drags down his or her mental energy to these affections, and forces reason to become the servant of the passions, there takes place a sort of perversion of the good mold of a human being into the irrational image, one's whole nature being traced anew after that design, just as if the reasoning mind were cultivating the beginnings of one's passions, and gradually multiplying them; for once reason lends its cooperation to passion, it produces a plenteous and abundant crop of evils.

Thus our love of pleasure took its beginning from our likeness to the irrational creation, but was increased by human transgression, generating many varieties of hedonistic sins such as we cannot even find among the irrational animals. Thus the rising of anger in us is indeed akin to the impulse of irrational animals; but it grows by alliance with rational thinking: from that come wrath, envy, deceit, conspiracy, and hypocrisy. All of these are the result of the evil cultivation of the mind; for if the passion is divested of the aid it receives from rational thinking, the anger that is left behind is short-lived and not sustained, like a bubble, perishing straightway as soon as it comes into being. Thus the greediness of pigs introduces covetousness, and the high-spiritedness of the horse becomes the origin of pride; and all the particular forms that proceed from the want of reason in irrational nature become vice by the evil use of the mind.

So conversely, if reason instead assumes sway over such emotions, each of them is transmuted to a form of virtue; for anger yields courage, terror caution, fear obedience, hatred aversion to vice, the power of love the desire for what is truly beautiful; high-spiritedness in our character raises our thought above the passions, and keeps it from bondage to what is base. The great Apostle, even, praises such a form of mental elevation when he bids us constantly to "set our minds on things that are above" (Col 3:2); and so we find that every such initiative, when elevated by loftiness of mind, is conformed to the beauty of the divine image.

But the other impulse is greater, as the tendency of sin is heavy and downward; for the ruling principle[9] of our soul is more inclined to be dragged downwards by the weight of the irrational nature than is the heavy and earthy element to be exalted by the loftiness of the intellect; hence the misery that encompasses us often causes the divine gift to be forgotten, and spreads the passions of the flesh, like some ugly mask, over the beauty of the image.

Those, therefore, are in some sense excusable who do not admit, when they look upon such cases, that the divine form is there; yet we may behold the divine image in human beings through those who have ordered their lives aright. For if the person who is subject to passion, and carnal, makes it incredible that humanity was adorned, as it were, with divine beauty, surely the person of lofty virtue and pure from pollution will confirm you in the better conception of human nature.

For instance (for it is better to make our argument clear by an illustration), one of those noted for wickedness—some Jechoniah for example,[10] or some other figure of evil memory—has obliterated the beauty of human nature by the pollution of wickedness; yet in Moses and in people like him the form of the image

---

9. Though Gregory's anthropology and moral psychology owe much to Platonism, he also regularly uses Stoic notions, such as the idea that the mind is the "ruling principle" (*hēgemonikon*) governing a human being's psychological constitution and life.

10. I.e., Jehoiachin (2 Kgs 24:8–15).

was kept pure. Now where the beauty of the form has not been obscured, there is made plain the faithfulness of the saying that the human being is an image of God.

It may be, however, that someone feels shame at the fact that our life, like that of the irrational animals, is sustained by food, and for this reason deems human beings unworthy of being supposed to have been framed in the image of God. But such a one may expect that freedom from this ingestive function will one day be bestowed upon our nature in the life we look for; for as the Apostle says, "the Kingdom of God is not food and drink" (Rom 14:17); and the Lord declared that "one shall not live by bread alone, but by every word that proceeds from the mouth of God" (Matt 4:4). Further, since the resurrection holds forth to us a life equal with the angels, and with the angels there is no food, there is sufficient ground for believing that human beings, who will live in like fashion with the angels, will be released from such a function.

7.3 Evagrius of Pontus, *To Eulogius*[11]

3. Let him who is beginning to attain to such virtue consider the warfare that is launched against it, lest, caught without training, he be easily dragged down as one unprepared. Therefore, the practice of ascetic labors is praiseworthy when there is peace, but bravery in these is eminently praiseworthy when warfare arises. Genuine virtue consists in bringing forth perseverance as one's weapon, not only for those circumstances in the course of which one is engaged in ascetic labors, but also for those evils in the course of which one is engaged in warfare; for impossible is the person who through very many battles has conquered passion, but caught in passions is the one who says he has acquired virtue without warfare. For the evil of the opposing forces is ranged against the battle line of the virtuous army of ascetic labors. The heart that does not have experience of warfare is deprived of the

---

11. Translated by Robert Sinkewicz, *Evagrius of Pontus: The Greek Ascetic Corpus*, Oxford Early Christian Studies (Oxford: Oxford University Press, 2003), 31, 40. Reprinted by permission of the Oxford University Press.

state of virtue, for "virtue" (*aretē*) is the name of the action that comes from the word "deeds of valor" (*aristeia*).

Virtue does not seek people's plaudits, for it takes no delight in honor, the mother of evils. Human esteem then is the beginning of honor and its end is pride, for the person who demands honors exalts himself and such a one does not know how to bear contempt. Desire for honor is a fantasy leading to pride, for he who is in love with it imagines for himself even an office.[12] Let the ascetic labor of the virtues be an honor for you and praise according to your will a dishonor. Do not seek the glory that comes from the flesh, you who dissolve the passions of the flesh; seek after the good, and it will be your glory.

He who wishes to be honored envies the one who surpasses him in fame and by this jealousy he piles up hatred towards his neighbors; overcome by too many honors, he wishes no one to be honored above himself and he snatches away the first prize, for fear that he appear inferior. He does not tolerate an esteemed man who is honored when he is absent, and even in the ascetic labors of the latter he seeks to ridicule his lowly esteem. An offence is a truly mortal wound for the person who loves esteem and he can find no escape at all from the wrath that comes of it. Such a person is the slave of a barbarian mistress and has been sold to many masters—pride, jealousy, envy, and the aforementioned elite among the spirits, but he who thrashes the spirit of honor with humility will destroy the entire legion of demons (cf. Mark 5:9; Luke 8:30); he who by humility presents himself to all as a servant will become like to the one who humbled himself and took the form of a servant (Phil 2:7).

If you measure yourself by the lowest measure, you will not compare your measure to another. The person who discloses the weakness of his soul by his lamentations will not hold a high opinion of the ascetic labors he undertakes for himself, nor will he even give his attention to the faults of others; rather, such a person must find assurance in a different way. The demons bring degradation and offence upon the humble so that they will flee from humility, unable to bear the contempt, but the person who

---

12. I.e., the temptation of clerical office, with the status that it entailed.

nobly bears dishonors with humility is all the more impelled by them towards the height of philosophy.

14. When you fight against the causes of the passions to put them to flight, do not at that moment let a thought exalt you in its treachery, lest perchance you put your confidence in a spirit of deceit and lose your mindfulness. Seek to scrutinize the suggested reasons for which you labor at ascesis, lest the goals of your attainments become corrupted through interior thoughts. Some people, lauded for their achievements, in time neglected ascetic labors, and their fame passed away and their ascetic labors were undone. Others endured hardship on account of the burden of the vices and were highly regarded; their soul's conscience was torn apart, the disease of fame spread abroad, the thoughts led the soul astray from its wounds and bore away its ascetic labors in the midst of praises. When those most practiced in ascetic labors receive a wealth of human honors, then the demons devise and introduce dishonors, so that, distanced from honors, they cannot bear dishonors nor can they tolerate offences.

Whenever you offer a great repentance for sins, then the thoughts, by magnifying the struggles of your ascetic efforts, make light of your sins and often conceal them with forgetfulness, or else they indicate that they are forgiven, so that, giving up on your ascetic labors, you do not take account of your failings so as to lament all the more over them. He who fights to cut off the passions that attack him will bring to the battle armed soldiers more numerous than the passions. Do not forget that you have fallen, even if you have repented, but hold onto the memory of your sin as an occasion of compunction that leads to your humility, so that thus humbled you will by necessity disgorge pride. . . .

7.4 John Cassian, *Conference* 5[13]

5. [Abba Serapion said]: "While these eight vices have diverse origins and variant influences, the first six—namely gluttony, fornication, greed, anger, dejection, and acedia—are connected with each other by a certain kindred relation and chain-linking, as it were, such that the overrun of the prior one effects the beginning of the next one. For from an excess of gluttony inevitably arises fornication; from fornication, greed; from greed, anger; from anger, dejection; from dejection, acedia. So we must combat all these by a similar method and the same plan, and it behooves us to attack the consequent passion through the one that precedes it. It is easier for a tree that is dangerously wide and tall to wither away if the roots that support it are first exposed and cut; and an infested pond of water will be dried up when its original source and the streams that feed it are skillfully occluded. This is why, in order to vanquish acedia, one must first overcome dejection; in order to cast out dejection, one must first drive out anger; in order to extinguish anger, you must trample down greed; in order to eradicate greed, you must curb fornication; in order to demolish fornication, you must castigate the vice of gluttony.

"Certainly the two remaining vices, namely vainglory and pride, are connected just like the vices we have mentioned, the overgrowth of the first prompts the beginning of the second (for an overrun of vainglory foments pride). But these two are altogether different from the first six vices, and are not associated in the same category with them since not only do they not take their rise from them but they are even aroused in a contrary manner and order. For when the six others have been eradicated, these two spring up and become all the more vivacious from their extinction. Thus we are assaulted by these two vices in a different manner. For we fall prey to one of the other six vices when we have been overcome by the ones that respectively precede them; but we are in danger of incurring these two when we are victorious and especially after our triumphs. All vices, there-

---

13. Translated from the Latin text edited by Petschenig, *Ioannis Cassianis Opera* II, Corpus Scriptorum Ecclesiasticorum Latinorum, vol. 13, 129–31.

fore, come out of the overgrowth of the ones that precede them, and are eradicated when the preceding ones are abated. For this reason, vainglory must be choked off for pride to be eliminated. Always when we overcome the prior ones, their successors fall idle, and by exterminating the prior ones, the remaining passions waste away without effort. Even though the eight vices which we have mentioned are connected and intermingled according to the scheme that we have discussed, they are, in particular, divided into four pairs. Fornication has a unique alliance with gluttony; anger is closely joined with greed; acedia with dejection; and pride with vainglory."

7.5 Diadochus of Photiki, *Chapters on Spiritual Knowledge*[14]

62. More than the other passions, ire disquiets and confuses the soul. But other times it does her a great service. Indeed, when used without agitation against the impious and every sort of libertine, whether to save or confound them, we obtain an extra dose of meekness for our souls since we necessarily converge with our goal: the justice and goodness of God. Further, by allowing ourselves to get deeply angered by sin, we often become even more virile wherever there is something of the effeminate. Nor should we doubt that though we are despondent and tremble before the Devil's boasting, we nonetheless show contempt before the spirit of corruption. To teach us this, our Lord's spirit was agitated and rebuked hell twice (John 12:27; 13:21)—although all that he undertook, he accomplished with serenity and singularity of purpose: he returned Lazarus's soul to his body (John 11:33) and so makes me believe that our God and Creator did well to equip our nature with anger to be used moderately as a weapon. If only Eve would have used it against the serpent she would not have been subjected to her sensual pleasure.

Thus it seems to me that whoever is found to use measured

---

14. Translated by Cliff Ermatinger, *Following in the Footsteps of the Invisible: The Complete Works of Diadochus of Photikē* (Collegeville, MN: Liturgical Press/Cistercian Publications, 2010), 96–97, 126–27. Used by permission of Liturgical Press. All rights reserved.

anger with religious zeal will tip the scale of retribution in his own favor, compared with another mind which, out of sluggishness, is unmoved by anger. This second person clearly has an untrained charioteer for a mind, while the former is a warrior borne by the horses of virtue and skilled in the four-horse chariot of self-mastery and the fear of God amid devils in battle array. This is the chariot of Israel about which we find written in Sacred Scripture regarding the assumption of the divine Elijah because it seems that God spoke distinctly to the Jews first about the four virtues.[15] Precisely for that reason, that child of wisdom was wholly taken up in a chariot of fire, so it seems to me, much as the temperate person controls his personal virtue as if they were horses, when he was taken up by the spirit in the wind of fire (2 Kgs 2:11). . . .

98. Impassibility does not consist in not being attacked by demons, because then we would all have to depart from this world, as the Apostle says (1 Cor 5:10), but in remaining undefeated when we are attacked by them. Thus, the iron-armored warriors sustain the shots of their enemies, hear the report of the shot, and they even see almost all of the arrows shot at them, but they are undefeated when attacked thanks to the solidity of their battle armor. They are dressed for battle and trust in the iron that protects them. But as regards us, covered in the armor of the holy light, with the helmet of salvation (Eph 6:11, 17), let us destroy the dark phalanxes of demons through our good works. For sure, it is not merely our not committing evil which makes us pure, but our forceful rejection of things evil through our attention to the good.

99. When the godly person is victorious over nearly all of his passion, two demons await to fight against him. One oppresses his soul terribly, bringing her from a great love for God to indiscreet zeal to such an extent that she does not want others to please God as much as she. The other demon moves about the body with a type of burning sensation that seeks carnal union. This begins in the body because this pleasure is proper to our

---

15. I.e., the four cardinal virtues now taken over into Christian morality: prudence, justice, temperance, and courage.

nature for procreation, and, therefore, one is easily overcome by it after that, as God allows. For when God sees that one of his warriors begins to flourish with a great amount of virtues, he lets him be stained by such a demon in order that he recognize himself as the vilest of worldly men. Indeed, this stirring up of passions occurs after good actions or even precedes them, so that through this being preceded or followed by passion, one seems somewhat useless to oneself (cf. Luke 17:10), regardless of his merits. We fight better against the first of these demons with much humility and love; and against the second we fight with self-mastery, the restraint from anger, and deep thoughts about death, so that in sensing the Holy Spirit's unceasing action, we become, in the Lord, masters of these passions.

7.6 Prudentius, *Psychomachia*[16]

From the western bounds of the world had come [the Virtues'] foe Indulgence (*Luxuria*), one that had long lost her repute and so cared not to save it; her locks perfumed, her eyes shifting, her voice listless, abandoned in voluptuousness she lived only for pleasure, to make her spirit soft and nerveless, in wantonness to drain alluring delights, to enfeeble and undo her understanding. Even then she was languidly belching after a night-long feast; for as it chanced dawn was coming in and she was still reclining by the table when she heard the hoarse trumpets, and she left the lukewarm cups, her foot slipping as she stepped through pools of wine and perfumes, and trampling on the flowers, and was making her drunken way to the war. Yet it was not on foot, but riding in a beauteous chariot that she struck and won the hearts of the admiring fighters. Strange warfare! No swift arrow is sped in flight from her bowstring, no lash-thrown lance shoots forth hissing, her hand wields no menacing sword; but as if in sport she throws violets and fights with rose-leaves, scattering baskets of flowers over her adversaries. So the Virtues are won over by her charms; the alluring breath blows a subtle poison

---

16. Lines 310–61, 371–418, translated by H. J. Thomson, *Prudentius* I, Loeb Classical Library, vol. 387 (Cambridge, MA: Harvard University Press, 1949), 301–5, 305–9. Reprinted by permission of Harvard University Press.

on them that unmans their frames, the fatally sweet scent subduing their lips and hearts and weapons, softening their iron-clad muscles and crushing their strength. Their courage drops as in defeat; they lay down their javelins, their hands, alas! enfeebled, all to their shame struck dumb in their wonder at the chariot gleaming with flashing gems of varied hue, as with fixed gaze they look longingly at the reins with their tinkling gold-foil, the heavy axle of solid gold, so costly, the spokes, one after another, of white silver, the rim of the wheel holding them in place with a circle of pale electrum. And by this time the whole array, its standards turned about, was treacherously submitting of its own will to a desire to surrender, wishing to be the slaves of Indulgence, to bear the yoke of a debauched mistress, and be governed by the loose law of the pot-house. The stout-hearted Virtue Soberness (*Sobrietas*) mourned to see a crime so sore, her allies deserting the right wing, a band once invincible being lost without shedding of blood. Like the good leader she is, she had carried the standard of the cross at the head of her troops, and now she plants the spike in the ground and sets it up, and with biting words restores her unsteady regiment, mingling appeals with her reproaches to awake their courage: "What blinding madness is vexing your disordered minds? To what fate are you rushing? To whom are you bowing the neck? What bonds are these (for shame!) you long to bear on arms that were meant for weapons, these yellow garlands interspersed with bright lilies, these wreaths blooming with red-hued flowers? Is it to chains like these you will give up hands trained to war, with these bind your stout arms, to have your manly hair confined by a gilded turban with its yellow band to soak up the spikenard you pour on, and this after you have had inscribed with oil on your brows the signs whereby was given to you the king's anointing, his everlasting unction? . . .

"Have you forgotten, then, the thirst in the desert, the spring that was given to your fathers from the rock, when the mystic wand split the stone and brought water leaping from its top? Did not food that angels brought flow into your fathers' tents in early days, that food which now with better fortune, in the lateness of time, near the end of the world's day, the people eats from the body of Christ? And it is after tasting of this banquet that you let shameful debauchery carry you relentlessly to the drunken den of Indulgence, and soldiers whom no raging Wrath nor idols could force by war to yield have been prevailed on by a tipsy dancer! Stand, I pray you. Remember who ye are, remember Christ too. Ye should bethink yourselves of your nation and your fame, your God and King, your Lord. Ye are the highborn children of Judah and have come of a long line of noble ancestors that stretches down to the mother of God, by whom God himself was to become man. Let the renowned David, who never rested from the troubles of war, awake your noble spirits; and Samuel too, who forbids touching the spoil taken from a rich foe, nor suffers the uncircumcised king to live after his defeat, lest the captive, were he allowed to survive, summon the victor from his life of peace to a renewal of war. He counts it sin to spare the monarch even as a prisoner; but your desire, on the contrary, is to be conquered and submit. Repent, I beseech you by the fear of the high God, if at all it moves you, that you have desired to follow after this pleasant sin, committing a heinous betrayal. If ye repent, your sin is not deadly. Jonathan repented that he had broken the sober fast with the sweet honeycomb, tasting, alas! in an evil hour the savor of honey on his rod, when the tempting desire to be king charmed his young mind and broke the holy vow. Yet because he repented we do not have to lament the fate that was decreed, and the cruel sentence did not stain his father's axe. Lo, I, Soberness, if ye make ready to concert with me, open up a way for all the Virtues whereby the temptress Indulgence, for all her great train, shall pay the penalty, she and her regiment, under the judgment of Christ." So speaking, she holds up the cross of the Lord in face of the raging chariot-horses, thrusting the holy wood against their very bridles; and for all their boldness they have taken fright at its outspread arms and flashing top, and in the rout of blind panic career down a steep place. Their driver, leaning far back and pulling on the reins, is carried helplessly along, her dripping locks befouled with dust; then she is thrown out and the whirling wheels entangle her who was their mistress, for she falls forward under the axle and her mangled body is the brake that slows the chariot down. Soberness gives her the death-blow as she lies, hurling at her a great stone from the rock.

8.

Love: Beginning and End of the Christian Virtues

INTRODUCTION

Historically, love (*agapē*; *caritas*) has been celebrated as the preeminent of the so-called "theological virtues" alongside faith and hope (1 Cor 13:13), and while patristic authors normally did not, like Thomas Aquinas, speak of love as a "supernaturally infused" virtue, they certainly exalted it as the virtue by which human beings most reflect God's own transcending virtue. It is little wonder, then, that there are numerous encomiums on love in early Christian literature, and in a variety of genres. Among the earliest is the selected passage from *1 Clement* [8.1], traditionally attributed to the bishop Clement but more likely the work of an anonymous representative of the church in Rome at the end of the first century. This passage reveals the extraordinarily early impact of Paul's own encomium on love in 1 Corinthians 13.

Numerous early Christian preachers and writers insisted that the Christian's love of God took an especially potent and concrete form in the love of the poor, to the extent that God manifested himself in the faces and bodies of the indigent. All three of the Cappadocian Fathers wrote sermons on Christian response to poverty, as did other bishops of late antiquity, including John

Chrysostom, but Gregory of Nazianzus's *Oration* 14 (*On the Love of the Poor*) remarkably exhibits the emphasis on loving God through loving the poor [8.2]. Gregory fully dramatizes the tragic plight of the poor and diseased (especially lepers), who were not just natural objects of public sympathy but often scorned and systematically alienated in Roman society. He uses various arguments (e.g., our solidarity with those who struggle with the caprices of bodily health; our common humanity, etc.), but his principal goal is to move Christians beyond mere recognition of their deprivations and to reach out to them in tender mercy and material aid, acknowledging each one as bearing the presence of Christ.

The richness of the love of God and love of neighbor was not, however, restricted totally to *agapē*. Beginning especially with Origen, in his *Commentary on the Song of Songs*, a whole series of early and medieval Christian authors refocused on the moral and spiritual power of *erōs*, "erotic" love transmuted into a godly passion or desire to be united with God and, by extension, with God's creatures. In the selection from his first *Homily on the Song of Songs* [8.3], Gregory of Nyssa not only justifies the conversion of the erotic language of the Song into an allegory of the soul's (bride's) relentless pursuit of the divine Logos (Bridegroom), he also makes clear that this deep-seated and fervent desire for God is necessary to bring about the "fullness of virtue." Gregory implies that this godly *erōs*, which launches and energizes the soul for intimacy with God, also has benefits for the moral life of the believer since no one can attain moral perfection apart from a radically transformed inner life. They are of a piece in the process of being fully assimilated to God.

John Chrysostom, who lionized the apostle Paul in many of his sermons and writings, including a whole series of homilies in praise of the apostle, insisted that Paul not only wrote eloquently of love as the chief of virtues but also concretely demonstrated that same love in his own ministry, even with his enemies and tormenters [8.4]. For Chrysostom, Paul was thoroughly justified in commanding his fellow believers to be his imitators, to the extent that he himself was imitating Christ (1 Cor 11:1).

In the same period as Chrysostom, Augustine made the love

of God and neighbor a true centerpiece of his theology, earning him the epithet *doctor caritatis* among Latin patristic authors. I can offer here only three samples of Augustine's teaching on love as the capstone of the virtues, but they are substantial ones. The passage from book 1 of his treatise *On Christian Doctrine* [8.5.1] appears in the larger context of explaining his distinction between things "enjoyed" for their own sake, preeminently the triune God, and things "used" in the attainment of worthy objects of desire (the ultimate such object being God). Though some of his modern critics are put off by his claim that we even "use" other human beings as tributary to the "enjoyment" of God rather than for their own sake, Augustine sees no problem, since loving one's neighbors, like loving oneself, is best shown in seeking to draw them, with oneself, toward the love of God and into the loving company of those who enjoy God, which is true happiness.

The second text of Augustine, from his *Enchiridion [Handbook] on Faith, Hope, and Love* [8.5.2], reinforces the principle whereby love is properly basic and internal to the other theological virtues, faith and hope, and is also the end of all the commandments. Given the quandary in the preceding text about "using" others for the enjoyment of God, Augustine here speaks of "the love of our neighbor in God," which means loving one's neighbors here and now by faith, and then, later, rejoicing when their own love and virtue comes to fruition in God.

Our third passage from Augustine comes in one of his *Homilies on 1 John* [8.5.3] and accentuates still another crucial dimension of love in his theology—the love that God "is" (1 John 4:7b–8), that thrives among the Persons of the Trinity, and that is also "of God" (1 John 4:7a) or from God in reaching out to include human beings in its communion. This is what frames a favorite scriptural text of Augustine's, Romans 5:5, with its testimony that "God's love has been poured into our hearts through the Holy Spirit which has been given to us." This point is important to Augustine's whole ethics, for the person who does not have or share this divinely authored love is effectively mocking God himself and quenching his Spirit.

If there is a *doctor caritatis* of the early Christian East to parallel

Augustine in the West, the Byzantine monk Maximus the Confessor (580–662) is an indisputable candidate. While for Maximus, narcissistic "self-love" (*philautia*) is the primal human vice, love itself, both as *agapē* and *erōs*, is the "cosmic virtue" that binds together creatures great and small, universal and particular, in the universe. It is the virtue par excellence in which the Logos "incarnates" or embodies himself in the virtuous Christian. The selections from Maximus's *Chapters on Love* (comprising four "centuries" or groups of one hundred epigrams) [5.6.1] reveal some of his major emphases: for instance, that love must be fully dispositional, a habit of the soul that both informs other virtues and completes all virtue; that love is tied up with *apatheia*, the ultimate stabilization of the passions; that the ardor of *erōs*, as passionate love of God (and, by extension, neighbor) serves *agapē*; that all people are to be loved *equally* by the Christian; and that love lies at the very core of cosmic reconciliation among all created beings. In his encomium on love in *Letter* 2, Maximus instructs an imperial official, John the Chamberlain, in the polymorphic nature of love, reiterating its comprehension of all the virtues and power to uproot vice (especially the original vice, self-love) and exalting its role in deifying the believer. For Maximus, as much as for Augustine, love is the beginning and end of the virtuous life.

THE TEXTS

8.1 *1 Clement*[1]

49. Let the one who embraces love in Christ perform Christ's commandments.[2] Who can explain the bond of God's love? Who can sufficiently declare the splendor of its beauty? The height to which love rises is ineffable. Love unites us to God. Love covers a multitude of sins (1 Pet 4:8). Love endures all things, and is patient in all things (1 Cor 13:4, 7). There is

---

1. Translated from the Greek text edited by Michael Holmes, *The Apostolic Fathers*, 3rd ed., 110–12.
2. Cf. John 14:15, 21; 15:10; 1 John 5:2–3; 2 John 1:6.

nothing vulgar, nothing arrogant in love (cf. 1 Cor 13:4–5). Love does not abide divisions; love sows no discord; love does everything in harmony. In love all God's chosen were perfected; without love there is nothing pleasing to God. In love the Master took hold of us. Because of the love he had for us, Jesus Christ our Lord gave his blood for our sake according to God's will; he also gave his flesh for our flesh, his life for our lives.

50. You see, beloved, how great and wondrous love is, how its perfection is impossible to describe. Who is adequate to be found in its embrace save those whom God deems worthy? Therefore let us pray for and beseech his mercy, so that we may be found faultless in love, free of human partiality. All the generations descended from Adam up to now have passed away, but those who were perfected in love by the grace of God have a place among the godly. They will be manifested when the kingdom of Christ appears (cf. 1 Pet 2:12; Luke 19:14). For it is written, "Enter into the inner chamber for a little while, until my anger and wrath have abated, and I shall remember a good day and shall raise you from your tombs" (Isa 26:20; Ezek 37:12). Blessed are we, beloved, if we keep performing God's commandments in the harmony of love, so that through love our sins may be forgiven us. For it is written, "Blessed are those whose transgressions are forgiven, and whose sins are covered. Blessed is the one of whose sin the Lord will not keep account, and in whose mouth there is no deceit" (Ps 32:1–2; Rom 4:7–8, 9). This blessedness comes upon those who have been chosen by God through Jesus Christ our Lord, to whom be the glory for ages unto ages. Amen.

8.2 Gregory of Nazianzus, *Oration* 14
(*On the Love of the Poor*)[3]

5. If, persuaded by Paul and by Christ himself, we must accept love as the first and greatest of the commandments, since it sums up the Law and Prophets (Matt 22:36–40), I find its best expres-

---

3. Translated from the Greek text in J.-P. Migne, ed., *Patrologia Graeca*, vol. 35 (Paris: J.-P. Migne, 1857), cols. 864B–865B, 868A–C, 894B–C, 908A, 909B–C.

sion to be the love of the poor, along with visceral mercy[4] and compassion for our fellow human beings. For of all things, God heals by nothing as much as by mercy, since nothing is more proper to God, whose "mercy and truth" precede him (Ps 89:14), and for whom we must offer our own mercy rather than justice (cf. Luke 6:35–38). By nothing else more than by loving-kindness will he who measures out his mercy using his scale and balance justly requite us with his own loving-kindness.

6. We must, then, open our tender mercies[5] to all the poor, and to all who suffer disasters of whatever cause, for according to the commandment we are "to rejoice with those who rejoice and weep with those who weep" (Rom 12:15). We must offer kindness as a gift to fellow human beings, whether their need is because of widowhood, orphanhood, displacement from their homeland, the cruelty of tyrants, the temerity of rulers, the inhumanity of tax-collectors, the brutality of robbers, the violent greed of thieves, confiscation of their property, or shipwreck. All alike are in need of mercy, looking to our hands for help in the same way as we ourselves look to God whenever we are in need of things. And of these victims, those who have suffered disaster beyond what they deserve are even more in need of mercy than those who suffer chronic misfortune. In particular are those ravaged by the sacred disease[6] that consumes them right down to their flesh, bones, and marrow—a condition threatening some persons in Scripture (cf. Ps 38:3; 102:3–5; Job 33:19–22). These victims are being betrayed by this deceptive, wretched, and faithless body. How I got yoked with this body, I do not know; nor do I know how, as an image of God, I got mixed up with this vessel of clay, which, even when it is in good condition, wages war against me, and when itself is embattled brings me distress. I love it as my fellow-servant and elude it as my enemy! I flee from it as if it were a chain and reverence it as my joint heir. I struggle to disband it, and yet I have no other

---

4. I have translated the Greek *eusplanchnia* as "visceral mercy," being the gut-level compassion ascribed to Jesus himself (cf. Matt 9:36; 14:14; 15:32; 20:34; Luke 7:13). This fits with Gregory's strongly incarnational language throughout the oration.

5. The Greek *splanchna* here can be variously translated "tender mercies," "bowels of mercy," "affection" (cf. Phil 1:8; 2:1; Col 3:12).

6. I.e., leprosy.

coworker to employ in my quest for excellence, knowing what I was created for and that I must ascend to God through my bodily actions. . . .

7. But now, in being pained over my own carnality and my own weakness reflected in the sufferings of others, reason prompts me to say this: brothers and sisters, we must care for those who share our human nature and our bodily slavery. For even if I accuse the body of being an enemy because of suffering, I also embrace it as my friend because of the one who made it my companion. And we must each care no less for the bodies of our neighbors than our own, whether they be healthy or consumed by this same disease. For we all are one in the Lord (cf. Rom 12:5), rich or poor, slave or free (Gal 3:28), healthy or unhealthy in body, and there is one Head from whom all things come: Christ (Col 2:19). What members are to each other, each of us is to other individuals, everyone to everyone (cf. Rom 12:5). So then, we must not overlook or neglect those who fall victim to our common weakness before we do, nor must we love the fact that we have good bodily health more than we lament that our brothers and sisters are languishing. We must consider that there is a single stability for our bodies and souls, which is showing those people loving-kindness. Let us further examine what I am saying.

8. For these other persons, only one thing determines their pitiable lot: the lack of something. Perhaps time, or stressful labor, or a friend or relative, or a change of circumstances has taken that thing away. But for these people [lepers], what is no less pitiful, if not more pitiful, is the fact that, in addition to lacking the ability to work and help themselves acquire the necessities of life, they lose their very flesh as well. For them the fear of growing weaker is always greater than the hope for health, and so for them there is little aid in hope, being the one real medication for the unfortunate. Besides their poverty itself, there is the second evil of disease, the most abominable and grievous of evils and for many people the easiest to identify as a curse. The third horror lies in the fact that these people are unapproachable, that most persons will not even look on them and instead avoid

them, considering them loathsome, like an evil to be averted. What is more grievous for them than their disease itself is when they sense that they are despised for their misfortune. I do not bear the suffering of these people without shedding tears, and I am confounded in recollecting it. May you feel the same way, so that with your own tears you might banish their tears. . . .

9. Give help! Offer food! Share clothing! Contribute medicine! Bind up wounds! Ask her about her misfortune! Provide him wise counsel about perseverance! Instill courage! Draw near in solidarity! Certainly you will not debase yourself by doing so; nor will you catch their disease, even if extremely squeamish persons think they might do so, duped by groundless reports—or rather, they use contagiousness as an excuse either for their cautiousness or their impiety, resorting to cowardice as though it were something noble and wise. Let the words of those trained by physicians, and the healers who dwell with these suffering people, convince you that no one who has come close to these people has run a risk. As for you, servant of Christ devoted to God and full of loving-kindness, even if you are dealing with a fearful situation, worthy of precaution, do not give in to such a sordid attitude. Be confident in your faith. Let compassion conquer your cowardice, the fear of God your weakness. Let piety hold firm in the face of your concerns for the welfare of your flesh. . . .

10. Let us therefore be cleansed by showing mercy. Let us wash away the filth and defilement of our souls with mercy's lovely soap. Let us make ourselves white, some of us "white as wool" (Isa 1:18) and others "white as snow" (Isa 1:18; Ps 51:7) in proportion to our visceral mercy. I tell you something that should strike greater fear in you. If you do not have a fracture, or a "bruise" or "festering wound" (Isa 1:6), or a leprosy of the soul, or sign of infection, or spot on the skin, all of which the Law did little to heal and which need Christ's healing touch, you must at least revere him who was wounded and bore infirmity for our sake—and you will show such respect if you are kind and loving to one who is a member of Christ (1 Cor 6:15). . . .

11. If, then, I am at all persuasive, fellow servants of Christ, brothers and sisters and joints heirs (cf. Rom 8:17; Eph 3:6), let us, while the time is ripe, visit Christ. Let us care for Christ. Let us feed Christ. Let us clothe Christ. Let us welcome Christ in (Matt 25:35). Let us honor Christ, not simply with food, as some do (Luke 7:36); nor with ointments, like Mary (John 12:3); nor only with a tomb, like Joseph of Arimathea (Matt 27:57–60); nor merely with items needed for burial, like the half-hearted friend of Christ Nicodemus (John 19:38–39); nor with gold, frankincense, and myrrh, like the Magi (Matt 2:11) who were there before all these others. Rather, since the Lord of all "desires mercy, and not sacrifice" (Hos 6:6; Matt 9:13), and since "visceral mercy is worth more than a myriad of fat rams" (Dan 3:40, Old Greek), let us bring this gift to Christ through the poor who today are cast to the ground, so that when we are set free from this world they may welcome us into the "eternal tabernacle" (Luke 16:9) in Christ himself, our Lord to whom be glory for all the ages. Amen.

8.3 Gregory of Nyssa, *Homily 1 on the Song of Songs*[7]

Let us then come within the holy of holies, that is, the Song of Songs. For we are taught by this superlative form of expression that there is a superabundant concentration of holiness within the holy of holies, and in the same way the exalted Word promises to teach us mysteries by the agency of the Song of Songs. For although there are many songs within the divinely inspired teaching, through which—from the great David and Isaiah and Moses and many others—we are instructed in noble thoughts about God, from this title we learn that the mystery contained in the Song of Songs transcends these songs of the saints by as much as they stand apart from the songs of profane wisdom. Human nature can neither discover nor entertain anything greater than this for purposes of understanding. This is why, moreover, the most intense of pleasurable activities (I mean

---

7. Translated by Richard Norris, *Gregory of Nyssa: Homilies on the Song of Songs*, Writings from the Greco-Roman World, no. 13 (Atlanta: Society of Biblical Literature, 2012), 29, 33, 41–42. Reprinted by permission of the Society of Biblical Literature.

the passion of erotic love) is set as a figure at the very fore of the guidance that the teachings give: so that by this we may learn that it is necessary for the soul, fixing itself steadily on the inaccessible beauty of the divine nature, to love that beauty as much as the body has a bent for what is akin to it and to turn passion into impassibility, so that when every bodily disposition has been quelled, our mind with us may boil with love, but only in the Spirit, because it is heated by that "fire" that the Lord came to "cast upon the earth." ...

The bride Moses kissed the Bridegroom [the divine Word] in the same way as the virgin in the Song who says, "Let him kiss me with the kisses of his mouth" (Song 1:2), and through face-to-face converse accorded him by God (as the Scripture testifies [cf. Num 12:8]), he became more intensely desirous of such kisses after these,[8] praying to see the Object of his yearning as if he had never glimpsed him. In the same way, all of the others in whom the divine desire is deeply lodged never ceased from desire; and everything that came to them from God for the enjoyment of the Object of yearning they made into the material and fuel for a more ardent desire. And just as now the soul that is joined to God is not satiated by her enjoyment of him, so too the more abundantly she is filled up with his beauty, the more vehemently her longings abound. ...

"That is why," she says, "young maidens have loved you [the Bridegroom], they have drawn you" (Song 1:3). She [the soul] speaks about the praiseworthy desire and of the disposition of love. For who is there without desire for such a Beauty, if only he has an eye capable of gazing upon its splendor? And while the beauty so discerned is great, that which such perception images and hints at is a thousandfold greater. But just as erotic love of the material order does not affect those who are still young (for childhood has no place for this passion) and one cannot see extremely old people afflicted in this way, so too in the case of the divine Beauty one still a child "tossed to and fro and carried away by every wind of doctrine" (Eph 4:14), and the elderly person who has aged and is approaching dissolution are both unmoved by this desire. For such people are not touched by

---

8. I.e., the theophanies that Moses experienced on Mt. Sinai in Exodus.

the invisible Beauty, but only a soul of the sort that has passed through the condition of childhood and has arrived at the height of spiritual maturity without receiving any "spot or wrinkle or any such thing"—the soul that is neither imperceptive by reason of youth nor weakened by old age. This soul our text calls a "young maiden," and she is faithful to "the first and great commandment" of the law. With her whole heart and strength she loves that Beauty whose description and form and explanation the human mind fails to discover. "Young maidens" of this sort, then, who have made increase by practice of the virtues and have already participated in the mysteries of the inner divine chamber as their youthfulness prescribes, love and delight in the beauty of the Bridegroom and through love turn to themselves. For this Bridegroom returns the love of those who love him. Speaking in the person of Wisdom he says, "I love those who love me" (Prov 8:17), and then, "With those who love me I share what I possess" (and *he* is her possession), "and I will fill their treasure houses with good things" (Prov 8:21). Hence the souls draw to themselves the longing for the incorruptible Bridegroom, "going after the Lord God," as it is written (cf. Hos 11:10).

Now what awakens their love is the sweet scent of the perfume, toward which, as they run unceasingly, they stretch themselves out for what lies ahead, forgetting what lies behind (cf. Phil 3:13).[9] Hence it says: "We will run after you, toward the fragrance of your perfumed ointments" (Song 1:4). But it is those who do not yet possess the fullness of virtue and are still immature who promise that they will pursue the goal toward which the fragrance of the perfumes points them (for it says, "We will run . . . toward the fragrance of your perfumed ointments"); the more perfect soul, on the other hand, who has more eagerly "stretched out toward what lies ahead," already attains the goal for the sake of which the course is run and is reckoned worthy of the goods that the treasure house contains—which is why she for her part says, "The king brought me to the treasure house" (Song 1:4). For the soul that has desired to touch the Good with the tips of her lips and has laid hold on the Beautiful just to the

---

9. Phil. 3:13 proved a favorite text of Gregory, supporting his vision of the "perpetual striving" (*epektasis*) of souls for the infinite God, in these homilies and especially in his *Life of Moses*.

extent that the strength of her prayer indicates (she prayed, one might say, to be made worthy of a kiss through the illumination of the Word), this same soul, empowered by its success in slipping through to the interior of what thought cannot articulate, cries out her request that her running not be confined to the outer courts of the Good but that by the firstfruits of the Spirit (cf. Rom 8:23)—of which she was made worthy by the first gift of grace, that is, by a kiss—she may come to the inner shrine of paradise and search "the depths of God" (1 Cor 2:10) and, like the great Paul, see (as he says) invisible things and hear unspeakable words (cf. 2 Cor 12:2–4). . . .

8.4 John Chrysostom, *Homily 3 in Praise of St. Paul*[10]

1. The blessed Paul, demonstrating the strength of human zeal, and showing us on his own that we can fly up to heaven without the aid of angels, archangels, and other powers (cf. 2 Cor 12:1–4), at one point urges us to imitate Christ through his own example, saying, "Be imitators of me as I am of Christ" (1 Cor 11:1). But at another point he leaves himself out and draws them directly to God himself, saying, "Be imitators of God, like beloved children" (Eph 5:1). Next, indicating that nothing so achieves this imitation as looking after the common welfare, for the good of everyone, he adds, "Walk in love" (Eph 5:2). For this same reason saying "Be imitators of me," Paul goes on forthwith to discourse on love (1 Corinthians 13), showing that this greatest virtue renders us intimate with God. So too there are virtues inferior to love, all of them focused on our humanity, such as fighting against lust, battling with the belly, struggling with greed, or wrestling with anger. But loving—this is common to us and God alike. For this reason Christ said to pray for those who insult you, so that you may become like your Father in heaven (Matt 5:44–45).

2. Realizing that love is the chief of virtues, Paul expounded it with great precision. No one had such affection for his enemies

---

10. Translated from the Greek text edited by Auguste Piedagnel, Sources Chrétiennes, no. 300 (Paris: Cerf, 1982), 162–68, 178.

or did such good to those who plotted against him or suffered so much for the sake of those who vexed him. For he did not dwell on what he suffered but concentrated instead on the common human nature he shared with his tormentors, and the more vicious they were, the more he showed mercy on their insanity. Say that a father has a son who is mad. The more the distressed child lashes out and kicks at the father, the more the father feels pity and weeps for him. So too Paul projected the disease [of his tormenters] as a surge of demons who led these attacks against him, and in response raised his concern for them all the more.

3. Listen to how gently and compassionately he discusses with us those who on five occasions had scourged him, stoned him, bound him, thirsted for his blood, and longed every day to tear him apart (cf. 2 Cor 11:24). "I bear witness," he says, "that they have a zeal for God, but it is not enlightened" (Rom 10:2). Furthermore, trying to restrain some who were lashing back at them, he said, "Do not be proud, but reverent. For if God did not spare the natural branches, neither may he spare you" (Rom 11:20–21). Seeing the divine judgment impending against them, he did what was in his power, he wept unremittingly and grieved for them. He impeded those who wished to attack them and strove to find even just a shadow of an excuse for their behavior. When, moreover, he could not persuade them with his words because of their obstinacy and obduracy, he resorted to continuous prayer, saying, "Brothers and sisters, my earnest desire and prayer for them is for their salvation" (Rom 10:1). He tendered them good hopes, saying, "The gifts and the call of God are irrevocable" (Rom 11:29), so that they would not completely despair and die. Deeply concerned about all these things, Paul was profoundly exercised on their behalf, such as when he quotes, "The Deliverer will come out of Zion, and he will put away impiety from Jacob" (Isa 59:20; Rom 11:26). Observing these people's self-destruction left Paul greatly broken and wounded, wherefore he contrived many consolations for his pain, at one point saying, "The Deliverer will come out of Zion, and he will put away impiety from Jacob" and at another point, "So they too have been disobedient in order that, by the

mercy shown to you, they also may receive mercy" (Rom 11:31).
. . .

4. In his greatness, Paul was a more robust flame than anyone in the chief of goods: love. Just as when an iron cast into a fire becomes completely fiery itself, Paul too was set on fire with love, and became love through and through. Acting like a common father of the entire inhabited earth, he mimicked the love of our earthly parents; or rather, he exceeded them all because of his bodily and spiritual solicitudes, donating everything—possessions, words, body and soul—for those whom he loved. . . .

8.5 Augustine: Various Reflections on Love

8.5.1 *On Christian Doctrine*, Book 1[11]

1.22.20. Among all these things, then, those only are the true objects of enjoyment which we have spoken of as eternal and unchangeable. The rest are for use, that we may be able to arrive at the full enjoyment of the former. We, however, who enjoy and use other things are things ourselves. For a great thing truly is a human being, made after the image and likeness of God (Gen 1:26–27), not as respects the mortal body in which one is clothed, but as respects the rational soul by which one is exalted in honor above the beasts. And so it becomes an important question, whether human beings ought to enjoy, or to use, themselves, or to do both. For we are commanded to love one another: but it is a question whether human is to be loved by human for his or her own sake, or for the sake of something else. If it is for his or her own sake, we enjoy the person; if it is for the sake of something else, we use that person. It seems to me, then, that a human being is to be loved for the sake of something else. For if a thing is to be loved for its own sake, then in the enjoyment of it consists a happy life, the hope of which at least, if not

---

11. Translated by J. F. Shaw, *St. Augustine's* City of God *and* Christian Doctrine, Nicene and Post-Nicene Fathers, 1st series, vol. 2 (Edinburgh: T&T Clark, 1886), 527–28, 529–30. Revised and updated.

yet the reality, is our comfort in the present time. But a curse is pronounced on the one who places hope in humanity (Jer 17:5).

1.22.21. Neither ought anyone to have joy in himself, if you look at the matter clearly, because no one ought to love even himself for his own sake, but for the sake of him who is the true object of enjoyment. For a person is never in so good a state as when her whole life is a journey towards the unchangeable life, and her affections are entirely fixed upon that. If, however, she loves herself for her own sake, she does not look at herself in relation to God, but turns her mind in upon herself, and so is not occupied with anything that is unchangeable. And thus she does not enjoy herself at her best, because she is better when her mind is fully fixed upon, and her affections wrapped up in, the unchangeable good, than when she turns from that to enjoy even herself. Wherefore if you ought not to love even yourself for your own sake, but for his in whom your love finds its most worthy object, no other person has a right to be angry if you love him or her too for God's sake. For this is the law of love that has been laid down by divine authority: "You shall love your neighbor as yourself"; but, "You shall love God with all your heart, and with all thy soul, and with all thy mind" (Matt 22:37–39; cf. Lev 19:18; Deut 6:5): so that you are to concentrate all your thoughts, your whole life and your whole intelligence upon him from whom you derive all that you bring. For when Jesus says, "With all your heart, and with all your soul, and with all your mind," he means that no part of our life is to be unoccupied, and to afford room, as it were, for the wish to enjoy some other object, but that whatever else may suggest itself to us as an object worthy of love is to be borne into the same channel in which the whole current of our affections flows. Whoever, then, loves his neighbor aright, ought to urge upon him that he too should love God with his whole heart, and soul, and mind. For in this way, loving his neighbor as himself, one turns the whole current of his love both for himself and his neighbor into the channel of the love of God, which suffers no stream to be drawn off from itself by whose diversion its own volume would be diminished. . . .

1.26.27. Seeing, then, that there is no need of a command that every human being should love himself and his own body—seeing, that is, that we love ourselves, and what is beneath us but connected with us, through a law of nature which has never been violated, and which is common to us with the beasts (for even the beasts love themselves and their own bodies)—it only remained necessary to lay injunctions upon us in regard to God above us, and our neighbor beside us. "You shall love," he says, "the Lord your God with all your heart, and with all your soul, and with all your mind; and you shall love your neighbor as yourself. On these two commandments hang all the law and the prophets" (Matt 22:37–40). Thus the end of the commandment is love, which is twofold, the love of God and the love of our neighbor. Now, if you take yourself in your entirety—that is, soul and body together—and your neighbor in her entirety, soul and body together (for a human being is made up of soul and body), you will find that none of the classes of things that are to be loved is overlooked in these two commandments. For though, when the love of God comes first, and the measure of our love for him is prescribed in such terms that it is evident all other things are to find their center in him, nothing seems to be said about our love for ourselves; yet when it is said, "You shall love your neighbor as yourself," it at once becomes evident that our love for ourselves has not been overlooked.

1.27.28. Now that is a person of just and holy life who forms an unprejudiced estimate of things, and keeps his affections also under strict control, so that he neither loves what he ought not to love, nor fails to love what he ought to love, nor loves that more which ought to be loved less, nor loves that equally which ought to be loved either less or more, nor loves that less or more which ought to be loved equally. No sinner is to be loved as a sinner; and every human being is to be loved as a human being for God's sake; but God is to be loved for his own sake. And if God is to be loved more than any human, each human being ought to love God more than herself. Likewise, we ought to love another human being better than our own body, because all things are to be loved in reference to God, and another human being can have fellowship with us in the enjoyment of God, whereas our body cannot; for the body only lives through the soul, and it is by the soul that we enjoy God.

1.28.29. Further, all human beings are to be loved equally. But since you cannot do good to all, you are to pay special regard to those who, by the accidents of time, or place, or circumstance, are brought into closer connection with you. For, suppose that you had a great deal of some commodity, and felt bound to give it away to somebody who had none, and that it could not be given to more than one person; if two persons presented themselves, neither of whom had either from need or relationship a greater claim upon you than the other, you could do nothing fairer than choose by lot to which you would give what could not be given to both. Just so among men: since you cannot consult for the good of them all, you must take the matter as decided for you by a sort of lot, according as each man happens for the time being to be more closely connected with you.

1.29.30. Now of all who can with us enjoy God, we love partly those to whom we render services, partly those who render services to us, partly those who both help us in our need and in turn are helped by us, partly those upon whom we confer no advantage and from whom we look for none. We ought to desire, however, that they should all join with us in loving God, and all the assistance that we either give them or accept from them should tend to that one end. For in the theatres, dens of iniquity though they be, if a man is fond of a particular actor, and enjoys his art as a great or even as the very greatest good, he is fond of all who join with him in admiration of his favorite, not for their own sakes, but for the sake of him whom they admire in common; and the more fervent he is in his admiration, the more he works in every way he can to secure new admirers for him, and the more anxious he becomes to show him to others; and if he find any one comparatively indifferent, he does all he can to excite his interest by urging his favorite's merits: if, however, he meet with anyone who opposes him, he is exceedingly displeased by such a man's contempt of his favorite, and strives in every way he can to remove it. Now, if this be so, what does it become us to do who live in the fellowship of the love of God, the enjoyment of whom is true happiness of life, to whom all who love him owe both their own existence and the love they bear him, concerning whom we have no fear that anyone who comes to know him will be disappointed in him, and who desires our love, not for any gain to himself, but that those who love him may obtain an eternal reward, even himself whom they love? And hence it is that we love even our enemies. For we do not fear them, seeing they cannot take away from us what we love; but we pity them rather, because the more they hate us the more are they separated from him whom we love. For if they would turn to him, they must of necessity love him as the supreme good and love us too as partakers with them in so great a blessing.

8.5.2 *Enchiridion on Faith, Hope, and Love*[12]

117. And now as to *love*, which the Apostle declares to be greater than the other two graces, that is, than faith and hope (1 Cor 13:13), the greater the measure in which it dwells in a human being, the better is that one in whom it dwells. For when there is a question as to whether a human being is good, one does not ask what he believes, or what he hopes, but what he loves. For the one who loves aright no doubt believes and hopes aright; whereas the one who has not love believes in vain, even though her beliefs are true; and hopes in vain, even though the objects of her hope are a real part of true happiness; unless, indeed, she believes and hopes for this, that she may obtain by prayer the blessing of love. For, although it is not possible to hope without love, it may yet happen that a woman does not love that which is necessary to the attainment of her hope; as, for example, if she hopes for eternal life (and who is there that does not desire this?) and yet does not love righteousness, without which no one can attain to eternal life. Now this is the true faith of Christ of which the Apostle speaks, "which works by love" (Gal 5:6); and if there is anything that it does not yet embrace in its love, asks that it

---

12. Translated by J. F. Shaw, *On the Holy Trinity, Doctrinal Treatises, Moral Treatises*, Nicene and Post-Nicene Fathers, 1st series, vol. 3 (Edinburgh: T&T Clark, 1887), 274–75, 275–76. Revised and updated.

may receive, seeks that it may find, and knocks that it may be opened unto it (Matt 7:7). For faith obtains through prayer that which the law commands. For without the gift of God, that is, without the Holy Spirit, through whom love is shed abroad in our hearts (Rom 5:5), the law can command, but it cannot assist; and, moreover, it makes a person a transgressor, for one can no longer excuse oneself on the plea of ignorance. Now carnal lust reigns where there is not the love of God. . . .

118. All the commandments of God, then, are embraced in charity, of which the Apostle says: "Now the end of the commandment is love, out of a pure heart, and of a good conscience, and of faith unfeigned (1 Tim 1:5). Thus the end of every commandment is charity, that is, every commandment has love for its aim. But whatever is done either through fear of punishment or from some other carnal motive and has not for its principle that love which the Spirit of God sheds abroad in the heart (Rom 5:5), is not done as it ought to be done, however it may appear to us. For this love embraces both the love of God and the love of our neighbor, and "on these two commandments hang all the law and the prophets" (Matt 22:40), we may add the Gospel and the apostles. For it is from these that we hear this voice: The end of the commandment is charity, and God is love (1 Tim 1:5; 1 John 4:16). Wherefore, all God's commandments, one of which is, "You shall not commit adultery" (cf. Matt 5:27; Rom 13:9), and all those precepts which are not commandments but special counsels, one of which is, "It is good for a man not to touch a woman" (1 Cor 7:1), are rightly carried out only when the motive principle of action is the love of God, and the love of our neighbor in God. And this applies both to the present and the future life. We love God now by faith, then we shall love him through sight. Now we love even our neighbor by faith; for we who are ourselves mortal know not the hearts of mortal humans. But in the future life, the Lord "both will bring to light the hidden things of darkness, and will make manifest the counsels of the hearts, and then shall everyone have praise of God" (1 Cor 4:5); for every person shall love and praise in his or her neighbor the virtue which, that it may not be hid, the Lord himself shall bring to light. Moreover, lust diminishes as love grows, till the

latter grows to such a height that it can grow no higher here. For "greater love has no man than this, that a man lay down his life for his friends" (John 15:13). Who then can tell how great love shall be in the future world, when there shall be no lust for it to restrain and conquer? For that will be the perfection of health when there shall be no struggle with death.

8.5.3 *Homily 7 on 1 John*[13]

4. "Beloved, let us love one another." Why? Because this is a man's counsel? "Because love is of God" (1 John 4:7a). It is a strong commendation of love, to say that it is of God; but there is more to come, and let us listen with all our ears. "Love," he has said, "is of God; and everyone that loves is born of God, and knows God. He that loves not, knows not God." Why? "For God is love" (4:7b–8). My brother and sisters, what more could be said? If nothing else whatever in any other page of Scripture, and this were the one and only thing we heard from the voice of God's Spirit—"For God is love"—we should ask for nothing more.

5. See now, that to act contrary to love is to act contrary to God. Let no man say: "When I do not love my brother, I sin against a man"—note this well—"sin against a man is a small thing, it is only against God I may not sin." How can you not be sinning against God, when you sin against love? "God is love." The words are not mine. If it were I that said, "God is love," any of you might take offense, and say, "What was that? What did he mean, 'God is love'? God has given love, God has granted love"—"Love is of God: God is love." There, my brothers and sisters, is God's Scripture before you: this is a canonical Epistle, read in every nation, maintained by universal authority, on which the world itself has been built up. Here you are told by the Spirit of God, "God is love." Now, if you dare, act against God, and refuse to love your brother.

---

13. Translated by John Burnaby, *Augustine: Later Works*, Library of Christian Classics (Philadelphia: Westminster, 1955), 314–15. Reprinted by permission of Westminster John Knox Press.

6. But how do these two texts stand to one another? First, "Love is of God," and now, "God is love." God is Father, and Son, and Holy Spirit. The Son is God of God; the Holy Spirit is God of God; and these three are one God, not three Gods. If the Son is God, and the Holy Spirit is God, and the one in whom the Holy Spirit dwells is a lover; then God is love—but God because of God. In the Epistle, you have both: "Love is of God," and "God is love." Of the Father alone, Scripture never says that he is "of God." So when we read the words "of God," we must understand them either of the Son or of the Holy Spirit. And from the saying of the apostle: "The charity of God is spread abroad in our hearts through the Holy Spirit that is given to us" (Rom 5:5), we may understand that in love is the Holy Spirit. It is the Holy Spirit himself, whom evil men cannot receive, who is that fountain out of which Scripture says, "Let your fountain water be your own, and let no stranger share with you" (Prov 5:16). For all who love not God are strangers, Antichrists. Though they enter our churches, they cannot be counted among the sons of God: that fountain of life belongs not to them. The evil man as well as the good can possess baptism: the evil man as well as the good can possess the gift of prophecy. King Saul possessed it; he persecuted the saintly David and was filled by the spirit of prophecy and began to prophesy. The evil man as well as the good can receive the sacrament of the Body and Blood of the Lord; for such it is written: "he that eats and drinks unworthily, eats and drinks judgment to himself" (1 Cor 11:29). The evil man as well as the good can have the name of Christ, can be called a Christian; of such it is written: "They defiled the name of their God" (Ezek 36:20). All these sacraments may be possessed by the evil man; but to have charity and be an evil man is not possible. This therefore is the peculiar gift of the Spirit: he is the one and only fountain. To drink of it, God's Spirit calls you: God's Spirit calls you to drink of himself.

8.6 Maximus the Confessor: Various Instructions on Love

8.6.1 *Chapters on Love*[14]

1.1. Love is a good disposition of the soul whereby one esteems no created being above the knowledge of God. It is impossible to arrive at the habitude of this love if one has proclivity for earthly things.

1.2. Love springs from dispassion, dispassion from hope in God, hope from endurance and long-suffering, the two of these from holistic self-control, self-control from the fear of God, and fear of God from faith in the Lord.

1.3. Whoever has faith in the Lord fears punishment, while whoever fears punishment restrains the passions. Whoever restrains the passions endures afflictions, while whoever endures afflictions will possess hope in God. Hope in God extracts us from attachment to what is earthly, and the mind thus separated from it will possess love for God.

1.10. Whenever the mind, by the sheer passion of its love for God, becomes ecstatic, it has no sense of itself or of any created beings whatsoever. For being illuminated by divine and infinite light, it is imperceptive of everything created by God, just as the eye no longer sees the stars once the sun rises.

1.11. All the virtues cooperate with the mind in questing for divine love (*erōs*), above all pure prayer,[15] through which the mind flies up to God and moves beyond all created things.

1.13. Whoever loves God cannot help but also love every human being as himself, even if the passions of those who are not yet

---

14. Translated from the Greek text edited by Aldo Ceresa-Gastaldo, *Massimo confessore: Capitoli sulla carita* (Rome: Editrice Studium, 1963), 50, 52–54, 62, 92–94, 122, 174–76, 186, 200.

15. "Pure prayer" comes from Evagrius, designating prayer liberated from mental images of things and from worldly distractions, thriving on intimacy with the ineffable God.

purified disturb him. Therefore, when he sees their conversion and correction, he erupts in boundless and unspeakable joy.

1.17. Blessed is the one who has become able to love all human beings equally.

1.40. The work of love is to do good to one's neighbors out of a disposition [of love] as well as to show them long-suffering and patience; it is also to use everything with right reason.[16]

2.9. Human beings love each other, whether to their praise or blame, for these five reasons: for God's sake, like the virtuous person who loves everyone and the person not yet virtuous who loves the virtuous person; or for natural reasons, as parents love their children and vice versa; or because of vainglory, like the one who is praised loves the one doing the praising; or because of greed, like the one who loves the rich for a share of their trappings; or out of love of pleasure, like the one who cares only for his belly and genitals. The first motive is praiseworthy, the second neutral, and the rest subject to passions.

2.10. If you hate some people, while others you neither love nor hate, and others you love but only moderately, and still others you love very much, recognize from this inequality how far you are from perfect love, such as enjoins you to love all people equally.

2.59. Be on guard against self-love, the mother of vices,[17] which is an irrational affection for the body. For from self-love clearly spring the first three passion-inducing and carnal thoughts, namely gluttony, greed, and vainglory, which have their origins

---

16. Like Augustine (see above, 8.5.1 [*On Christian Doctrine* 1.22.20–21]), Maximus appropriates and Christianizes Stoic ethical teaching on "using" things for virtuous rather than vicious purposes, and according to "right reason" (*orthos logos*) which respects God's ordering of, and purpose for, all things. Maximus likely would have concurred with Augustine's idea of "using" another human being virtuously by loving them for God's own sake.

17. Various patristic authors speculated about the "original" vice that triggered the Adamic fall. Envy and pride were good candidates, but Maximus suggested "self-love," which can take a negative form, as here, but also a positive form, another point on which Maximus and Augustine intersected.

in supposedly necessary bodily needs. From these three, in turn, the entire catalog of vices comes about. So it is necessary, as I said, to guard against self-love and to fight it with much sober-mindedness, for when it is eradicated, all its vicious offspring are eradicated along with it.

3.67. Just as the simple thought of human concerns does not force the mind to spurn divine realities, neither does the subtle knowledge of divine realities persuade the mind fully to spurn human affairs, for the simple fact that truth at present subsists in shadows and hints. For this reason we need the blessed passion (*pathos*) of holy love (*agapē*) to bind the mind to spiritual objects of contemplation and to persuade it to prefer immaterial reality to the material, and intelligible and divine reality to empirical.

3.90. If you hold a grudge against anyone, pray for him and you will stifle the passion in its tracks. Through prayer you separate the hurt from the memory of the wrong he did you; and in becoming charitable and kind you totally dispel the passion from your soul. Conversely, if someone holds a grudge against you, be gracious and humble toward him, and deal fairly with him, and you will release him from his passion.

4.17. The objective of God's providence is to unify by right faith and spiritual love those who have been variously pulled apart by vice. Precisely for this purpose the Savior suffered, "in order that the dispersed children of God might be gathered into one" (John 11:52). Whoever, then, does not endure troubles, hold up under distress, or bear with toils walks outside God's love and the purpose of his providence.

8.6.2 Letter 2 (*To John the Chamberlain*)[18]

There is nothing having more the form of God, nothing more pregnant with mystery, nothing that elevates human beings higher toward deification, than divine love (*agapē*). For love

---

18. Translated from the Greek text in J.-P. Migne, ed., *Patrologia Graeca*, vol. 91 (Paris: J.-P. Migne, 1863), cols. 393B–396C, 397C–400A, 401C–D, 404B–C.

has gathered in itself all the beautiful things which the *logos* of truth accounts as being in the form of virtue, and separates itself completely from anything whatsoever that has the form of evil, since love is the fulfilment of the Law and the Prophets (Matt 22:36–40). The mystery of love supersedes them by making us gods out of human beings, and by reducing the individual precepts to their universal *logos*.[19] Within this *logos*, at God's good pleasure, they are encompassed in a single form, and through this *logos* love is generously distributed in many different ways according to the divine economy.

What possible form of the good does love not possess? Surely not faith, being the premier supposition of all acts of piety; faith, which provides the believer full assurance that God and divine realities do indeed exist; faith, which furnishes those who see with a judgment about empirical realities that goes beyond what the eye can supply when it observes their mere appearances. Surely not hope, which confirms in its own right the good that truly exists (cf. Heb 11:1) and holds on to it better than does the hand when it clutches the densest of material objects. Does not love give enjoyment of the things in which one believes and hopes, by dispositionally considering future things as already present? Surely love does not lack possession of humility, the primary foundation of the virtues whereby we come to know ourselves and are able to cut out the tumor of our own arrogance. Surely not meekness, through which we beat back censure and praise alike, and, from the diagonal line running between evils, namely between glory and ill-repute, we jettison vexation. Surely not gentle-spiritedness, whereby, amid suffering, we remain unchangeable toward those who do us wrong, in no way ill-disposed toward them. Surely not mercy, whereby we willingly take others' misfortunes on ourselves, and do not fail to ignore that they are of our same human nature and race. Surely not self-control and patience, long-suffering and goodness, peace and joy, all by which we gradually suppress ire and desire, along with their seething and fervency. Simply and concisely stated, love is the ultimate end of all good things,

---

19. Maximus uses *logos* here with regard to its embedded purpose, or the inherent principle whereby it serves the Creator's goal for creation and humanity.

since for God it is the summit of all goods and the basis of every good. Being trustworthy, infallible, and enduring, love guides and leads forward all who walk in its way (cf. Eph 5:2).

For faith is the foundation of whatever comes after it—namely, hope and love (cf. 1 Cor 13:13)—and provides a secure basis for what is true. Hope is the raw strength of the two others, love and faith, since, in its own right, hope discloses to both, respectively, what is lovable and what is believable, and it instructs the other two to hold to the same course through hope. Love, as the ultimate object of desire, is the fulfillment of faith and hope, since love fully enfolds the whole, and provides the other two stability of movement toward the same goal. Love in its own right introduces faith to a present enjoyment of what it believes in and hope to a present enjoyment of what it hopes for.
. . .

Self-love is, and is known as, the first sin, the Devil's first offspring, and the mother of the passions that succeed from it. Whoever, through love, is granted to be worthy of God, abolishes self-love and with it the whole mob of vices, which has no other basis or existential cause than self-love. The one who has abolished self-love no longer knows arrogance, the mark of conceit against God, a compound and bizarre vice. He knows nothing of the self-glory that causes one to fall, and that brings down one who is swollen with it. He dissipates envy, a passion that itself justly dissipates the one who is subject to it, by voluntarily befriending, with good will, his fellow human beings. He altogether uproots anger, the thirst for blood, wrath, guile, hypocrisy, pretense, vengefulness, greediness, and all the passions that fragment a unitary human being. For by extirpating self-love, being the origin, the mother of vices as I said, all the passions that derive from it and succeed it are usually extirpated as well. This is because once self-love is gone, nothing at all of evil, neither form nor trace, can survive, while all the forms of virtue are allowed to appear, fulfilling the power of love, such as gathers together what has been divided up, thus refashioning the human person once more to a single principle of being and mode of existence. This power of love equalizes and reconciles any intentional inequality and divergence between human beings, and, as it must, advances that commendable inequality whereby each person is drawn to his neighbor in preference to himself, and esteems that neighbor over himself, insofar as he is eager to spurn the former relation and to excel beyond it. . . .

Love, then, is a great good, and among good things the first and preeminent good, since, for the one who has it, love joins together God and humanity, and causes the very Creator of humanity to appear as human because of the pure likeness in the good of the deified human to God, insofar as that likeness is humanly attainable. As I understand it, this love induces one to love the Lord God with all one's heart and soul and might, and to love one's neighbor as oneself (cf. Deut 6:5; Luke 10:27). What this means, if I may give it a summary definition, is our universal and inherent relation to the primal Good, which carries with it the whole providential purpose of humankind so far as its nature is concerned. Nothing else can cause the lover of God to ascend any higher, since all other paths of true piety are subordinate to it. . . .

Because of this, the very Creator of nature himself—truly this is the most awesome thing ever heard of!—donned our human nature, uniting it to himself in person without compromising his divinity, that he might stabilize the humanity he bore, and ingather it to himself, such that, thus ingathered, our nature might have absolutely no divergence from him in its inclination.[20] And so he has made fully manifest the all-glorious way of love, truly divine and deifying and directing us toward God. . . .

---

20. "Inclination" (*gnōmē*) is a loaded term in Maximus's usage, but in this passage has the sense of the collective inclination or intention of individual human beings in their own moral willing and choosing.

Supplemental Bibliography

Babcock, William, ed. *The Ethics of St. Augustine*. Atlanta: Scholars Press, 1991.

Bayless, Grant. *The Vision of Didymus the Blind: A Fourth-Century Virtue-Origenism*. Oxford Theological Monographs. Oxford: Oxford University Press, 2015.

Behr, John. "Patristic Humanism: The Beginning of Christian Paideia." In *Re-Envisioning Christian Humanism: Education and the Restoration of Humanity*, edited by Jens Zimmermann, 19–32. Oxford: Oxford University Press, 2017.

Bejczy, István. *The Cardinal Virtues in the Middle Ages: A Study in Moral Thought from the Fourth to the Fourteenth Century*. Brill Studies in Intellectual History 202. Leiden: Brill, 2011.

Bénatouïl, Thomas, and Mauro Bonazzi, eds. *Theoria, Praxis and the Contemplative Life after Plato and Aristotle*. Leiden: Brill, 2012.

Benko, Stephen. *Pagan Rome and the Early Christians*. Bloomington: Indiana University Press, 1984.

Blowers, Paul. "Aligning and Reorienting the Passible Self: Maximus the Confessor's Virtue Ethics." *Studies in Christian Ethics* 26 (2013): 333–50.

———. "Emotional Scripts and Personal Moral Identity: Insights from the Greek Fathers." In *Personhood in the Byzantine Christian Tradition: Early, Medieval, and Modern Perspectives*, edited by Alexis Torrance and Symeon Paschalidis, 19–28. Aldershot: Ashgate, 2018.

———. "Envy's Narrative Scripts: Cyprian, Basil, and the Monastic

Sages on the Anatomy and Cure of the Invidious Emotions," *Modern Theology* 25 (2009): 21–43.

———. "Pity, Empathy, and the Tragic Spectacle of Human Suffering: Exploring the Emotional Culture of Compassion in Late Ancient Christianity." *Journal of Early Christian Studies* 18 (2010): 1–27.

Boersma, Hans. *Embodiment and Virtue in Gregory of Nyssa: An Anagogical Approach*. Oxford Early Christian Studies. Oxford: Oxford University Press, 2015.

Bradshaw, David. "Pagan and Christian Paths to Wisdom." In *The Bright and the Good: The Connection between Intellectual and Moral Virtues*, edited by Audrey Anton, 93–110. London: Rowman & Littlefield, 2018.

Brock, Sebastian, and Susan Ashbrook Harvey. *Holy Women of the Syrian Orient*. Transformation of the Classical Heritage 13. Berkeley: University of California Press, 1998.

Brown, Peter. *The Body and Society: Men, Women, and Sexual Renunciation in Early Christianity*. Rev. ed. New York: Columbia University Press, 2008.

———. "The Saint as Exemplar in Late Antiquity." *Representations* 2 (1983): 1–25.

Brown, William, ed. *Character and Scripture: Moral Formation, Community, and Biblical Interpretation*. Grand Rapids: Eerdmans, 2002.

Burridge, Richard. *Imitating Jesus: An Inclusive Approach to New Testament Ethics*. Grand Rapids: Eerdmans, 2007.

Byers, Sarah. "Early Christian Ethics." In *The Cambridge History of Moral Philosophy*, edited by Sacha Golob and Jens Timmermann, 112–24. Cambridge: Cambridge University Press, 2017.

———. *Perception, Sensibility, and Moral Motivation in Augustine: A Platonic-Stoic Synthesis*. New York: Cambridge University Press, 2013.

Chadwick, Henry. "Philosophical Tradition and the Self." In *Late Antiquity: A Guide to the Classical World*, edited by G. W. Bowersock, Peter Brown, and Oleg Grabar, 60–81. Cambridge, MA: Harvard University Press, 1999.

Clark, Elizabeth. *Reading Renunciation: Asceticism and Scripture in Early Christianity*. Princeton: Princeton University Press, 1999.

Colish, Marcia. *Ambrose's Patriarchs: Ethics for the Common Man.* Notre Dame, IN: University of Notre Dame Press, 2005.

Coon, Lynda. *Sacred Fictions: Holy Women and Hagiography in Late Antiquity.* Philadelphia: University of Pennsylvania Press, 1997.

Cooper, John. *Pursuits of Wisdom: Six Ways of Life in Ancient Philosophy.* Princeton: Princeton University Press, 2013.

Despland, Michel. *The Education of Desire: Plato and the Philosophy of Religion.* Chicago: University of Chicago Press, 1985.

Dihle, Albrecht. *The Theory of Will in Classical Antiquity.* Berkeley: University of California Press, 1982.

Driscoll, Jeremy. *Steps to Spiritual Perfection: Studies on Spiritual Progress in Evagrius Ponticus.* Mahwah, NJ: Paulist/Newman Press, 2005.

Ferguson, Everett, ed. *Christian Life: Ethics, Morality, and Discipline in the Early Church.* Studies in Early Christianity 16. New York: Garland, 1993.

Fitzgerald, John, ed. *Passions and Moral Progress in Greco-Roman Thought.* London and New York: Routledge, 2008.

Greer, Rowan. *Broken Lights and Mended Lives: Theology and Common Life in the Early Church.* University Park, PA: Pennsylvania State University Press, 1986.

Greer, Rowan, and J. Warren Smith. *One Path for All: Gregory of Nyssa on the Christian Life and Human Destiny.* Eugene, OR: Wipf & Stock, 2015.

Hadot, Pierre. *Philosophy as a Way of Life: Spiritual Exercises from Socrates to Foucault.* Translated by Arnold Davidson. Oxford: Blackwell, 2013.

———. *What Is Ancient Philosophy?* Translated by Michael Chase. Cambridge, MA: Harvard University Press, 2002.

Harakis, Stanley. *Wholeness of Faith and Life: Orthodox Christian Ethics.* Part 1, *Patristic Ethics.* Brookline, MA: Holy Cross Orthodox Press, 1999.

Harper, Demetrios. *The Analogy of Love: St. Maximus the Confessor and the Foundation of Ethics.* Yonkers, NY: St. Vladimir's Seminary Press, 2018.

Harrington, Daniel, and James Keenan, eds. *Jesus and Virtue Ethics: Building Bridges between New Testament Studies and Moral Theology.* Lanham, MD: Sheed & Ward, 2002.

———. *Paul and Virtue Ethics: Building Bridges between New Testament Studies and Moral Theology*. Lanham, MD: Sheed & Ward, 2010.

Hausherr, Irénée. *Penthos: The Doctrine of Compunction in the Christian East*. Translated by Anselm Hufstader. Kalamazoo, MI: Cistercian Publications, 1982.

Hays, Richard. *The Moral Vision of the New Testament: Cross, Community, New Creation*. San Francisco: HarperCollins, 1996.

Henten, Jan Willem van, and Joseph Verhyden, eds. *Early Christian Ethics in Interaction with Jewish and Greco-Roman Contexts*. Leiden: Brill, 2013.

Horn, Cornelia. "Penitence in Early Christianity in Its Historical and Theological Setting: Trajectories from Eastern and Western Sources." In *Repentance in Christian Theology*, edited by Mark Boda and Gordon Smith, 153–87. Collegeville, MN: Liturgical Press, 2006.

Humphries, Thomas. *Ascetic Pneumatology from John Cassian to Gregory the Great*. Oxford Early Christian Studies. Oxford: Oxford University Press, 2013.

Krueger, Derek. *Liturgical Subjects: Christian Ritual, Biblical Narrative, and the Formation of the Self in Byzantium*. Philadelphia: University of Pennsylvania Press, 2014.

Layton, Richard. *Didymus the Blind and His Circle in Late-Antique Alexandria: Virtue and Narrative in Biblical Scholarship*. Urbana: University of Illinois Press, 2004.

Leemans, Johan, Brian Matz, and Johan Verstraeten, eds. *Reading Patristic Texts on Social Ethics: Issues and Challenges for Twenty-First Century Christian Social Thought*. Washington, DC: Catholic University of America Press, 2011.

Lilla, Salvatore. *Clement of Alexandria: A Study in Christian Gnosticism and Platonism*. Oxford Theological Monographs. London: Oxford University Press, 1971.

Lohfink, Gerhard. *Jesus and Community*. Minneapolis: Fortress Press, 1984.

Longenecker, Richard, ed. *Patterns of Discipleship in the New Testament*. Grand Rapids: Eerdmans, 1996.

Luomanen, Petri, Anne Birgitta Pessi, and Ilkka Pyysiäinen, eds. *Christianity and the Roots of Morality: Philosophical, Early Christian, and Empirical Perspectives*. Leiden: Brill, 2017.

MacIntyre, Alasdair. *After Virtue: A Study in Moral Theory*. 3rd ed. Notre Dame: University of Notre Dame Press, 2007.
Malherbe, Abraham. *Moral Exhortation: A Greco-Roman Sourcebook*. Library of Early Christianity 4. Philadelphia: Westminster, 1986.
———. *Paul and the Thessalonians: The Philosophic Tradition of Pastoral Care*. Philadelphia: Fortress Press, 1987.
Martens, Peter W. *Origen and Scripture: Contours of the Exegetical Life*. Oxford Early Christian Studies. Oxford: Oxford University Press, 2012.
Matera, Frank. *New Testament Ethics*. Louisville: Westminster John Knox, 1996.
McDonald, J. Ian. *The Crucible of Christian Morality*. London: Routledge, 1998.
Meconi, David, ed. *Sacred Scripture and Secular Struggles*. The Bible in Ancient Christianity 9. Leiden: Brill, 2015.
Meeks, Wayne. *The Moral World of the First Christians*. Library of Early Christianity 6. Philadelphia: Westminster, 1986.
———. *The Origins of Christian Morality: The First Two Centuries*. New Haven: Yale University Press, 1995.
Murphy, Francis X., ed. *The Christian Way of Life*. Message of the Fathers of the Church 18. Wilmington, DE: Michael Glazier, 1986.
Newhauser, Richard, ed. *In the Garden of Evil: The Vices and Culture in the Middle Ages*. Papers in Medieval Studies 18. Toronto: Pontifical Institute of Mediaeval Studies, 2005.
Nock, A. D. *Conversion: The Old and the New in Religion from Alexander the Great to Augustine of Hippo*. London: Oxford University Press, 1933.
Nussbaum, Martha. *The Fragility of Goodness: Luck and Ethics in Greek Tragedy and Philosophy*. Rev. ed. Cambridge: Cambridge University Press, 1986.
———. *The Therapy of Desire: Theory and Practice in Hellenistic Ethics*. Princeton: Princeton University Press, 2009.
O'Donovan, Oliver. *The Problem of Self-Love in Saint Augustine*. New Haven: Yale University Press, 1980.
Okholm, Dennis. *Dangerous Passions, Deadly Sins: Learning from the Psychology of Ancient Monks*. Grand Rapids: Brazos, 2014.

Osborn, Eric. *Clement of Alexandria*. Cambridge: Cambridge University Press, 2005.

———. *Ethical Patterns in Early Christian Thought*. Cambridge: Cambridge University Press, 1976.

———. *Tertullian: First Theologian of the West*. Cambridge: Cambridge University Press, 1997.

Osborne, Catherine. *Eros Unveiled: Plato and the God of Love*. Oxford: Oxford University Press, 1996.

Prunet, Olivier. *La morale de Clément d'Alexandrie et le Nouveau Testament*. Paris: Presses Universitaires de France, 1966.

Rabbow, Paul. *Seelenführung: Methodik der Exerzitien in der Antike*. Munich: Kösel, 1954.

Rambaux, Claude. *Tertullien face aux morales des trois premiers siècles*. Paris: Les Belles Lettres, 1979.

Satran, David. *In the Image of Origen: Eros, Virtue, and Constraint in the Early Christian Academy*. Transformation of the Classical Heritage 58. Berkeley: University of California Press, 2018.

Sider, Robert D., ed. *Christian and Pagan in the Roman Empire: The Witness of Tertullian*. Washington, DC: Catholic University of America Press, 2001.

Smith, J. Warren. *Christian Grace and Pagan Virtue: The Theological Foundation of Ambrose's Ethics*. New York: Oxford University Press, 2010.

Sorabji, Richard. *Emotions and Peace of Mind: From Stoic Agitation to Christian Temptation*. Oxford: Oxford University Press, 2000.

———. *Moral Conscience through the Ages: Fifth Century BCE to the Present*. Chicago: University of Chicago Press, 2014.

Starr, James, and Troels Engberg-Pedersen, eds. *Early Christian Paraenesis in Context*. Berlin: Walter de Gruyter, 2005.

Thompson, James. *Moral Formation according to Paul: The Context and Coherence of Pauline Ethics*. Grand Rapids: Baker Academic, 2011.

Torrance, Alexis. "Individuality and Identity-Formation in Late Antique Monasticism." In *Individuality in Late Antiquity*, edited by Alexis Torrance and Johannes Zachhuber, 111–27. Burlington, VT: Ashgate, 2014.

———. *Repentance in Late Antiquity: Eastern Asceticism and the Framing of the Christian Life c. 400–650 CE*. Oxford Theology and Religion Monographs. Oxford: Oxford University Press, 2013.

Wetzel, James. *Augustine and the Limits of Virtue*. Cambridge: Cambridge University Press, 1992.

———. *Parting Knowledge: Essays after Augustine*. Eugene, OR: Cascade, 2013.

Wilken, Robert Louis. "Alexandria: A School for Training in Virtue." In *Schools of Thought in the Christian Tradition*, edited by Patrick Henry, 15–30. Philadelphia: Fortress Press, 1984.

———. "Christian Formation in the Early Church." In *Educating People of Faith: Exploring the History of Jewish and Christian Communities*, edited by John van Engen, 48–62. Grand Rapids: Eerdmans, 2004.

———. *The Christians as the Romans Saw Them*. 2nd ed. New Haven: Yale University Press, 2003.

———. "The Lives of the Saints and the Pursuit of Virtue." In *Remembering the Christian Past*, 121–44. Grand Rapids: Eerdmans, 1995.

———. *The Spirit of Early Christian Thought: Seeking the Face of God*. New Haven: Yale University Press, 2003.

Wogaman, J. Philip, and Douglas Strong, eds. *Readings in Christian Ethics: A Historical Sourcebook*. Louisville: Westminster John Knox, 1996.

Womer, Jan, ed. *Morality and Ethics in Early Christianity*. Sources of Early Christian Thought. Philadelphia: Fortress Press, 1987.

Index of Subjects and Names

(Page references include footnote content)

Abraham, 5, 26, 100, 104–5
Abraham of Qidun, 100–101, 110–14
acedia, 148, 149
Adam, 15, 71, 94–96, 101, 122, 159
Almsgiving (and care for the poor), 6, 51–52, 53, 55, 64, 65, 92, 120, 131–32, 156, 160–63
Ambrose of Milan, 15, 30, 100, 104, 120, 128
angels, 42, 46, 57, 65, 72, 80, 87, 110, 111, 125, 126, 145, 152, 166
anger: as righteous indignation, 77, 139–40, 149; as wrath or fury, 8, 23, 45, 47, 52, 53, 59, 66, 85, 86, 87, 108, 132, 138, 140, 142, 144, 148, 149, 149, 150, 151, 179, 180

apatheia (dispassion; impassibility), 22, 46, 140, 145, 150, 158, 164, 176
Aristides of Athens, 50, 54
Aristotle, 7, 8, 10, 137
arrogance, 43, 52, 54, 87, 133, 159, 179
Arsenius, Abba, 25
asceticism, 14, 87–88, 111, 112, 121, 139, 145–47. See also practice
Athenagoras of Athens, 35
Augustine of Hippo, 3–4, 7, 10, 15, 23, 71, 96, 120, 131, 156–57, 168

baptism, 3, 13, 14, 16, 22–23, 24, 25, 30, 32, 64, 100, 102–3, 109, 119–20, 122–28, 175
Basil of Caesarea, 7, 70, 84, 88, 100, 107
beauty, divine, 143, 144, 145, 158, 164–65
Benedict of Nursia, 7, 51, 66
body, 10, 18, 24, 30, 39, 42, 45,

46, 61, 62, 66, 75, 83, 108, 122, 124–25, 128, 142, 149, 150–51, 156, 160–61, 164, 168, 170–71, 177–78; diseased, 18, 156, 160, 161–62

Caesarius of Arles, 15, 32, 50–51, 64
Cassian, John, 6, 7, 15, 27, 139, 148
chastity, 17, 105
Christianity: growth and status in the Roman Empire, 2, 4, 35, 36, 38–39, 49; as moral leaven in the empire, 36, 38–39, 54–56; the name "Christian," 55, 61, 64, 108, 109, 175; normative identity of, 2; resistance to the empire, 35–37, 39–41, 41–42; as rule of life, 49–67
church, 5, 15–16, 23, 30–33, 37, 39, 49, 51, 53, 64–65, 70, 89, 103, 110, 115, 121; attendance at, 64–65
Cicero, 19, 100, 141–42
Clement of Alexandria, 6, 9, 50, 62, 70, 72, 73, 78
1 Clement, 155, 158
commandments, 1, 5, 16–17, 49, 50, 52, 53, 54, 55, 59, 60, 65, 80, 105, 127, 136, 137, 158, 159, 165, 168, 170, 173, 179
compassion, 113, 114, 132, 135, 162

compunction. *See* repentance
confession. *See* sin
conscience, 2, 3, 14, 15, 17, 50, 53, 58, 117, 135, 147, 173
Constantine, 4, 14, 35, 37, 70
contemplation (*theōria*), 6–7, 46, 72, 79, 84, 97, 121, 134, 178; of nature, 83
conversion. *See* repentance
Cyprian of Carthage, 36, 41
Cyril of Jerusalem, 119–20, 122

David, 31, 77, 78, 79, 100, 106–7, 129, 153, 163, 175
death: physical, 24, 38, 45, 56, 66, 72, 87, 88–89, 108, 125, 130, 132, 135, 141, 142, 151, 174; "second," 142; to self, 32, 120, 123, 127; spiritual, 50, 51, 54, 64, 115, 120
deification, 9, 81–82, 97, 133, 178, 179, 181
dejection, 148, 149. *See also* grief, as sorrow
demons, 47, 122, 135, 139, 146, 147, 150, 151, 167
desire, 9, 10, 25, 59, 73, 138, 142, 144, 164, 165, 179, 180. *See also* love, as *erōs*
detachment, 46–47
Devil (Satan), 16, 20, 23, 40, 50, 59, 61, 65, 120, 122, 124, 126, 149
Diadochus of Photiki, 139–40, 149
Didache, 49–50, 51, 120
diet. *See* food

INDEX OF SUBJECTS AND NAMES 193

Dionysius the Areopagite, Pseudo–, 121, 132
discipline. *See* asceticism; *paideia*, divine
dress, Christian, 50, 60–62

Elijah, 101, 109, 150
Elisha, 100, 130
emotion, 8, 71, 88, 111, 137–40, 141, 144, 169. *See also* passions; vice; virtue
envy, 8, 65, 87, 146, 177, 180
epektasis (perpetual striving), 165
Ephrem the Syrian, 71, 93
Epistle to Diognetus, 36, 38
erōs. *See* love
Eucharist, 3, 120, 128–31, 135, 152–53, 175
Evagrius of Pontus, 6, 7, 15, 26, 84, 139, 140, 145
Eve, 95, 149
exempla, 4–5, 49, 86, 99–117
exile, 37, 47–48, 106

faith, 1, 16, 22, 23, 24, 41, 42, 58, 72, 73, 76, 81, 97, 105, 109, 115, 124, 125, 127, 155, 157, 162, 172–73, 176, 178, 179, 180
faithfulness, 5, 50, 100, 106, 114, 145, 165
fall of humanity (Adamic fall), 8, 102, 125, 128, 136, 138, 177
fasting, 18, 46, 51, 55, 66, 109, 114, 120, 131, 132, 153

fear of God, 53, 61, 74, 76, 150, 153, 162, 176
food (and diet), 17, 18, 38, 39, 45, 47, 50, 55, 58, 63, 102, 106, 145, 152, 162, 163. *See also* gluttony
forgiveness, 19, 21, 25, 26, 30, 31, 65, 114, 159
formation. *See* liturgy; mimesis; morality; *paideia*, divine; *philosophia*
fornication, 148, 149. *See also* lust
fortitude (courage), 100, 107, 144, 162

gluttony, 50, 63, 148, 149, 177–78
grace, 10, 14, 15, 21, 50, 51, 65, 73, 74, 94, 97, 110, 115, 119, 120, 121, 123, 128, 130, 132, 159, 166, 172
greed, 52, 54, 105, 140–41, 143, 148, 149, 160, 166, 177–78, 180
Gregory of Nazianzus, 4, 7, 71, 89, 156
Gregory of Nyssa, 7, 37, 43, 70–71, 87–89, 138–39, 142, 163
Gregory Thaumaturgus, 70, 80, 82
Gregory the Great, 7, 101–2, 115
grief: as emotional pain, 21, 45, 59, 84, 109, 111, 113, 167; as sorrow, 55, 88–89, 160, 162

habitude (or disposition), 134, 137, 138, 158, 176, 177. *See also* virtue

hagiography, 5, 100–101

happiness, 8, 42, 58, 126, 128, 157, 168–69, 172

heart, 10, 16, 27, 28, 66, 141, 165, 169, 170, 173, 175, 181

Hezekiah, King, 114

holiness. *See* purity and purification

Holy Spirit, 23, 40, 41, 53, 59, 69, 81, 96, 115, 123, 124, 126, 127, 130, 151, 157, 164, 166, 173, 174, 175

honor, 8, 17, 32, 38, 42, 47, 87, 90, 139, 141, 146, 147, 168

hope, 20, 53, 54, 55, 66, 78, 88, 124, 127, 155, 161, 168–69, 172, 176, 179, 180

human nature, 9–10, 43, 44, 45, 128, 130, 142–45, 149, 150–51, 161, 163–64, 167, 179, 181. *See also* body; image of God; likeness to God; mind; soul; will

humility, 8, 17–18, 24, 47, 55, 87, 114, 137, 146–47, 151, 179

idolatry. *See* paganism

image of God, 9, 44, 70, 73, 74, 91, 138, 143, 144, 145, 160, 168. *See also* likeness to God

Irenaeus of Lyons, 9

Isaac, Abba, 27

Isaiah, 163

Jacob, 106

Jacob of Sarug, 15, 28

Jesus Christ: as divine wisdom, 69, 71, 96–98; as High Priest, 30, 72; as Image of God, 9; imitation of, 5, 36, 69, 99, 100, 101–2; incarnate or embodied, 3, 29, 96–98, 116, 129, 130, 158, 159, 163, 181; as Instructor and Logos, 62–63, 70, 72–73, 74–80; as Light, 29; "mind" of, 69; as Savior and Lord, 6, 27, 31, 50, 53, 57, 81–82, 108, 122, 123, 125, 127; suffering and crucified, 1, 64, 69, 72, 122, 123, 132, 153, 159, 178

Job, 5, 99, 100, 101–2, 106, 115–17

John Chrysostom, 7, 14, 15, 20, 37, 155–56, 166

John Climacus, 37, 45

John the Apostle, 31

John the Baptist, 101

Jonathan, 153

Joseph (patriarch), 106, 114

Joseph of Arimathea, 163

joy and enjoyment, 21, 24, 27, 31, 45, 73, 74, 90, 108, 113, 117, 125, 128, 133, 134, 157, 164, 168–69, 170–72, 177, 179, 180

Judas Iscariot, 109, 114, 115, 121, 135–36

INDEX OF SUBJECTS AND NAMES   195

judgment, divine, 18, 27, 42, 57, 66, 91–93, 117, 167. *See also* punishment, divine
justice (righteousness), 19, 54, 73, 74, 85, 100, 106, 107, 110, 116, 149

Kant, Immanuel, 2–3
knowledge: of God, 1, 23, 28, 54, 56, 62, 73, 79, 96–98, 107, 174, 176, 178; of good and evil, 71, 94–96

Lactantius, 14, 19, 138, 140
Lazarus, 46, 114, 115, 149
Lent, 120, 131–32
likeness (or assimilation) to God, 9, 44, 70, 73, 74, 138–39, 142, 143, 156, 168, 181. *See also* image of God
liturgy, 2, 3, 119–28, 131–36
love, 21, 38, 39, 46, 47, 75, 76, 79, 82, 106, 143, 155–81; as *agapē* (love of God and neighbor), 8, 51, 52, 55, 60, 66, 69, 73, 74, 96, 124, 131, 134, 144, 150, 151, 155–63, 164, 165, 166–81; as *erōs* (passionate love), 47, 156, 158, 163–64, 176; God's, 32, 75, 76, 79, 111, 114, 157, 158–59, 174–75, 178; of self, 8, 42, 158, 169, 170, 177–78, 180. *See also* compassion; desire; mercy
lust, 8, 19, 23, 40, 52, 54, 86, 105, 122, 140, 173–74

Macarius, Pseudo–, 14–15, 20
Macrina, 70, 87–89
Magi, 50, 57–58, 163
Mark the Monk, 14–15, 22, 140
marriage, 3, 17, 38, 130
martyrs and martyrdom, 36, 39–41, 41–42, 100, 107–10
Mary of Bethany, 163
Matoes, Abba, 25
Maximus the Confessor, 7, 10, 139, 158, 176
memory and remembrance, 2, 5, 47, 53, 93, 107, 124, 131, 153, 147, 178
mercy, 8, 16, 29, 53, 54, 55, 92, 101, 114, 125, 131, 132, 135, 136, 159, 160, 166, 168, 172, 179
mimesis, 4–5, 86, 87, 100–117, 119–28, 156, 166. *See also* exempla
mind, 9–10, 24, 28, 83, 84, 93, 116, 133, 134, 143, 144, 150, 152, 164, 169, 170, 176, 178
monks and monasticism, 6, 7, 8, 9, 15, 46, 47, 51, 67, 112, 121, 134, 139
morality, formation in, 2–3, 7, 8. *See also* mimesis; *paideia*, divine; *philosophia*
moral philosophy, 3, 6, 107. *See also philosophia*
moral psychology, 9–10, 140
moral reason, 3, 62, 74, 104–5, 139, 143, 161, 177
moral "use," 137–38, 139, 144, 149–50, 157, 168, 177

moral vision, 3, 137
Moses, 46, 75, 100, 101, 103, 130, 144, 163, 164

natural law, 43, 105, 170
Nicodemus, 163
Nilus of Ancyra, 101, 114

Origen, 6, 9, 36, 70, 73, 80, 82–84, 99–100

paganism (and idolatry), 3, 36, 50, 51, 52, 54–55, 56–60, 65–66, 73, 78, 97, 103, 138, 153
pagan learning and literature, Christian use of, 3, 70, 80–81, 84–86, 100
paideia, divine, 69–71, 74–80. See also Jesus Christ, as Instructor
Paradise, 20, 93–96, 108, 109, 110, 116, 122, 166
passions, 8, 19, 26, 45, 46, 48, 59, 60, 85, 88, 104, 105, 138, 139, 140, 142–43, 144, 145, 146, 147, 148, 149, 150, 151, 156, 158, 164, 176–77, 178, 180. See also apatheia; body; desire; emotion; *erōs*; soul; vice
patience, 5, 8, 53, 54, 65, 66, 106, 137, 177, 179
Paul the Apostle, 5, 7, 9, 22, 23, 24, 36, 41, 96–97, 102, 115, 117, 125, 144, 150, 156, 159, 166–68, 172, 173

perfection, 9, 22, 23, 51, 121, 132–34, 138, 159
Peter the Apostle, 31
philosophia, 6–7, 70–71, 80, 83–84, 85, 87–89, 147. *See also paideia*, divine
Plato and Platonism, 9, 85
pleasure, 22, 39, 45, 46, 59, 63, 66, 75, 85, 116, 132, 140, 141, 142, 143, 149, 150–51, 177
Poemen, Abba, 26
poor, the. *See* almsgiving
practice (*praxis*, virtuous conduct), 6–7, 22, 24, 46, 84, 86, 87, 90, 104, 105, 106, 127, 137, 165. *See also* asceticism
prayer, 18, 22, 25, 26, 27, 28, 30, 32, 33, 47, 51, 52, 53, 56, 64, 67, 81, 86, 87, 109, 110, 113, 114, 120, 122, 124–25, 128, 129, 131, 159, 164, 166, 167, 172, 173, 176, 178; Lord's Prayer, 51, 64; "pure," 176
pride, 8, 87, 139, 143, 146, 147, 148, 149, 177. *See also* vainglory
providence, divine, 75, 90–93, 178, 181
prudence, 5, 6, 74, 100, 107, 114. *See also* wisdom
Prudentius, 140, 151
punishment, divine, 18, 33, 38, 56, 76, 90–91, 93, 142; fear of, 18, 27, 47, 66, 173, 176. *See also* judgment, divine

INDEX OF SUBJECTS AND NAMES 197

purity and purification, 16, 17, 18, 29, 46, 52, 79, 89, 121, 132–34

reason. *See* moral reason
renunciation: of Satan in baptism, 126; of worldly things and evils, 37, 45–48, 66
repentance, 13–33, 93, 153; as compunction and tears, 15, 21, 25–30, 31, 45, 48, 66, 101, 113, 114, 117, 139, 147; ecclesial dimension of, 15–16, 18, 30–33; *exomologēsis* (public repentance) 14, 17–18, 33; as lifelong discipline, 14–15, 20–25, 32; *metanoia*, 13, 19; "second" repentance, 13–14, 16–20, 24
ritual. *See* baptism; Eucharist; liturgy; sacraments
Romanos the Melodist, 121, 135

sacraments, 2, 3, 102, 103, 119–20, 122–31, 133, 175. *See also* baptism; Eucharist
Samuel, 27, 153
Satan. *See* Devil
Saul, King, 27, 175
Sayings of the Desert Fathers, 25
Scripture: investigation of, 81; as medium of divine instruction (Word), 70, 75–80; as sacred narrative, 2, 99–100, 119; typological interpretation of, 99–101, 102–3, 114–15, 119–20. *See also* exempla
self-control, 6, 60, 106, 151, 170, 176, 179
Serapion, Abba, 148
Shepherd of Hermas, 13–14, 16
Simon Magus, 114, 115
sin and sins, 8, 14, 16–17, 18, 19, 20, 21, 22, 23, 26, 27, 31, 33, 45, 46, 52, 54, 56, 65, 75, 77, 78, 91, 112, 113, 115, 116, 117, 125, 144, 153, 159; confession of, 14, 17–18, 26, 30–31, 33, 66. *See also* fall of humanity; vice
slaves and slavery, 37, 43–45, 53, 55, 106
sobriety, 55, 61, 62, 64, 140, 152–54, 178
Solomon, 43, 76, 78, 79, 81, 115, 123
soul, 9–10, 19, 24, 26, 27, 29, 30, 39, 42, 45, 53, 59, 62, 70, 88, 90, 112, 113, 115, 122, 132, 136, 139, 140, 141, 142, 144, 146, 147, 149, 150, 156, 161, 162, 164–65, 166, 168, 169, 170, 171, 178, 181. *See also* human nature; mind
spectacles (theatre), 50, 58–60, 171
Stoicism, 9–10, 137–38, 144, 177

tears. *See* repentance

temper, 9
temperance, 85, 100, 107
temptation, 16, 23, 131, 139, 146, 153
Tertullian of Carthage, 14, 36, 39, 50, 56
Theodore of Mopsuestia, 120, 124
thoughts (*logismoi*), 22, 50, 139, 147, 151, 169
tribulations (sufferings, testings), 22, 28, 42, 46, 91, 110, 123, 124, 125, 161, 162, 167, 176, 179

vainglory, 47, 148, 149, 177
vice, 5, 7–8, 19, 54, 101, 137–54, 158, 178, 180. *See also* passions; sin and sins
virtue, 5, 6, 7–8, 26, 33, 84–85, 90, 100, 101, 105, 137–54, 165, 166, 173; "theological virtues" (faith, hope, love), 155, 157, 172–74, 176, 179, 180. *See also* habitude

will, 3, 10, 47, 54, 67, 78, 111, 152, 180, 181; freedom of, 10, 19, 40, 43, 44, 71, 75, 138; of God, 8, 10, 57, 73, 130, 159; self-will, 47, 52, 54
wisdom, 5, 7, 47, 70, 71, 84, 89–90, 96–98, 111–12. *See also* moral reason; *philosophia*; prudence

Index of Scriptural References

(Page references include footnote content)

Genesis
1:1–2:1	129
1:26	43, 44, 73, 91
1:26–27	9, 138, 142, 168
2:9	94
2:17	94
2:25	122
3:7	94
3:21	108
12:1–4	104
12:11–13	105
14:14	105
15:4	105
17:15	105
25:34	106
27:42	106
33:4	106
39	106

Exodus
3:18–19	75
11:2	80
12:35–36	80
14:21–22	130
14:22	102
14:29	102
15:23–25	130
15:25	29
16:4–36	129
16:13–15	102
17:11–13	46
20:1–17	50
20:3–6	55
20:12	54
20:13–14	52
20:14	54
20:15	52
20:15–16	64
20:16	52, 54
20:17	52, 54
25:40	80
32:1–35	78
34:28	109

Leviticus
19:12	86
19:18	51, 169

INDEX OF SCRIPTURAL REFERENCES

Numbers
12:8   164

Deuteronomy
5:2   86
6:5   51, 169, 181
28:39   92
30:1–5   78–79
32:5–6   77

Joshua
3:15–17   102

2 Samuel
1:21   92

1 Kings
6:1   115
11:14–22   81
12:28   81
19:8   109

2 Kings
2:11   150
6:5–6   130
24:8–15   144

Job
3:1–4   101
3:3–4   115–17
3:4   116
33:19–22   160

Psalms
(by Hebrew enumeration)
1:1   78, 79
1:3   79
1:4   79
6   28
6:6   27
8:7–8   43
16:7   116
18:44–45   77
31:5   26
32:1–2   159
33:9   129
38:3   160
42:2–3   27
48:8   78
49:18   59
50:21   91
51:7   29, 162
65:9   92
78:23–25   129
78:24   102
79:12   91
82:6   74
89:14   160
102:1   28
102:3–5   160
102:9   27, 31
103:2–5   132
104:14   44
111:10   90
114:5–6   103
114:7–8   103
115:3   108
119:91   43
119:136   31
120:5–6   27
129:7   91
143:2   27

Proverbs
1:7   76
3:11–12   76
3:13   79

5:16	175	5:8–9	75–76
8:4	78	6:9	79
8:6	78	6:10	76
8:17	165	6:16	79
8:21	165	9:1	27
16:31	90	17:5	169
23:3	63	17:16	116

Ecclesiastes

2:7	43, 45
3:2	123

Lamentations

1:1–2	77
2:18	27

Song of Songs

1:2	164
1:3	164
1:4	165
5:3	122

Ezekiel

2:6–7	75
18:21–23	78–79
33:11	78–79
36:20	175
37:12	159

Isaiah

1:2	76
1:4	76, 77
1:6	162
1:18	162
3:14	93
5:8	92
5:10	92
10:3	91
10:22–23	90
26:20	159
29:21	93
30:1	76
40:2	91
43:2–3	102–3
58:7	131
59:20	167

Daniel

3:40	163

Hosea

6:6	163
11:10	165

Amos

2:7	93
5:10	93

Habakkuk

1:16	93

Haggai

1:9	92

Jeremiah

2:12–13	76
3:3–4	77

Zechariah

11:5	93

Malachi		11:12	46
3:8	92	11:28	79
		11:28–30	73
Wisdom of Solomon		13:31	79
9:15	24	16:18	29
		16:26	44
Sirach		18:14	21
7:23–24	75	19:21	58
12:1–7	52	19:29	58
		21:1–7	73
Baruch		21:8–11	73
3:13	79	22:36–40	159, 179
		22:37–39	51, 169
Matthew		22:37–40	170
2:1	57	22:40	173
2:11	163	23:27	90
2:12	50, 57	23:33	77
4:2	109	23:37	75
4:4	145	23:37–39	77
5:3	28, 58	25:35	163
5:5	53	26:14–15	131
5:21–22	23	27:9	131
5:26	52	27:27	108
5:27	173	27:35	108
5:28	23, 86	27:57–60	163
5:39	51, 86		
5:41	51	Mark	
5:44	60, 86	5:9	146
5:48	51		
6:12	25	Luke	
6:24	58	4:2	131
6:25	58	6:20	58
6:28	58	6:21	31
7:7	81, 173	6:27–28	51
7:12	55	6:29	51
8:12	78	6:30	51
9:13	163	6:32–33	51
10:28	42	6:35	51
10:38	58	6:35–8	160

INDEX OF SCRIPTURAL REFERENCES

9:62	58	12:27	149
7:11–17	31	13:13–14	131
7:36	163	13:21	149
7:36–50	28	14:6	131
7:38	30	14:15	158
8:30	146	14:21	158
10:27	181	15:10	158
12:18	93	15:13	174
12:59	52	15:18–19	36
14:27	58	19:28	131
14:28–29	58	19:38–39	163
15:4–32	101		
15:15	21	Acts	
16:9	163	1:26	109
17:10	151	2:38	13, 16
18:14	131	9:1–30	109
18:22	58	9:36–42	31
19:14	159	15:1	1
19:41	27		
22:41–44	131	Romans	
22:62	31	1:18	97
		1:23	97
John		2:15	117
1:5	29	3:24	3
1:11	132	4:7–8	159
1:14	97	4:9	159
4:7	131	5:5	157, 173, 175
4:44	47	6:5	130
6:31–35	129	6:11	3
6:35	131	6:23	3
6:54	131	8:1–2	3
8:12	29	8:16–17	41
8:44	23	8:17	163
9:5	29	8:23	166
10:3	81	8:39	3
11:33	149	9:28	90
11:52	178	10:1	167
12:3	30, 163	10:2	167
12:25	42	11:17–24	122

INDEX OF SCRIPTURAL REFERENCES

11:20–21	167	12:7–8	96
11:26	167	13	155, 166
11:29	44, 167	13:3	155
11:31	168	13:4	158
11:36	54	13:4–5	159
12:5	3, 161	13:7	158
12:14	60	13:13	172, 180
12:15	160	14:8	89
13:9	173	14:19	89
14:17	145	15:54	24
16:3	3		
16:7	3	2 Corinthians	
		2:1–4	166
1 Corinthians		3:6	9
1:11–13	1	4:1–5:21	5
1:18–2:9	69	4:4	36
1:24	69	5:6–7	24
1:30	3, 69	5:17	89, 120, 129
2:6	36, 90	6:16	115
2:8	36	6:17	47
2:10	166	11:16–33	5
2:10–16	69	11:24	167
3:22	114, 115	11:29	131
4:5	173	12:2–4	166
4:9	110	12:9	131
4:10	3		
4:15	3	Galatians	
4:17	3	1:1	109
5:10	150	3:28	161
6:13	63	4:3	36
6:15	162	5:6	172
7:1	173		
7:8	17	Ephesians	
8:1–13	55	3:6	163
8:4	55	4.13	1
8:6	54	4:14	164
10:11	103, 115, 119	4:22	108, 122
11:1	5, 156, 166	4:24	89
11:29	175	4:30	40

INDEX OF SCRIPTURAL REFERENCES 205

4:30–31	59	6:1–2	22
5:1	166	6:4–6	23
5:2	166, 180	9:24	73
5:6	93	10:26	23
6:11	150	11:1	179
6:17	150	12:3–13	69
		13:15	89

Philippians

2:7	131, 146	1 Peter	
2:11	125	2:11	51
3:10	123	2:12	159
3:13	165	4:8	158
4:8	7		

2 Peter

Colossians

1:16	54	1:4	82
2:1–3	96		
2:9	131	1 John	
2:15	122	2:6	41
2:19	161	2:15–17	36
3:2	144	4:7a	157, 174
3:9	122	4:7b–8	157, 174
		4:16	173
		5:2–3	158

1 Thessalonians

4:13	88	2 John	
4:17	102	1:6	158
5:17	22		

Revelation

1 Timothy

		2:11	142
1:5	173	5:4	31
6:20	1	14:9–11	42
		17:4	32

Hebrews

		20:6	142
1:2	54	20:14	142
3:14	82	21:8	142
4:4–10:31	30		

www.ingramcontent.com/pod-product-compliance
Lightning Source LLC
Chambersburg PA
CBHW020408080526
44584CB00014B/1233